DATE			

The Experimenter's Guide
to Solid-State Diodes

The Experimenter's Guide to Solid-State Diodes

Robert J. Traister

Prentice-Hall, Inc., Englewood Cliffs, N.J. 07632

Library of Congress Cataloging in Publication Data

TRAISTER, ROBERT J.   (date)
  The experimenter's guide to solid-state diodes.

  Includes index.
  1. Diodes, Semiconductor—Handbooks, manuals, etc.
I. Title.
TK7871.86.T65 1983   621.3815'22   83-3088
ISBN 0-13-295444-3

Editorial/production supervision
  and interior design: *Gretchen K. Chenenko*
Cover design: *Edsal Enterprises*
Jacket design: *Jeannette Jacobs*
Manufacturing buyer: *Anthony Caruso*

Printed in the United States of America

10 9 8 7 6 5 4 3 2 1

ISBN   0-13-295444-3

Prentice-Hall International, Inc., *London*
Prentice-Hall of Australia Pty. Limited, *Sydney*
Editora Prentice-Hall do Brasil, Ltda., *Rio de Janeiro*
Prentice-Hall Canada Inc., *Toronto*
Prentice-Hall of India Private Limited, *New Delhi*
Prentice-Hall of Japan, Inc., *Tokyo*
Prentice-Hall of Southeast Asia Pte. Ltd., *Singapore*
Whitehall Books Limited, *Wellington, New Zealand*

Contents

6 Solid-State Diode Projects *74*

Preface

Although solid-state diodes are used in nearly every type of electronic circuit, whether simple or complex, one rarely comes across a projects book that deals exclusively with these devices. Today, many persons sing the praises of the transistor and the integrated circuit and tell how these devices have revolutionized the electronics industry. Although I cannot argue with this point and in fact agree with it wholeheartedly, I still insist that the solid-state diode, in all of its many configurations, has not been given the credit it so richly deserves.

In these modern times, electronic hobbyists and experimenters think nothing about quickly throwing together an ac-derived dc power supply. All you need is a transformer and a couple of solid-state rectifiers, and you're there. If you want voltage regulation, then add a zener diode or two. A few decades ago, however, this would have been a herculean task. Instead of fitting a few components on a tiny piece of circuit board and connecting them to the transformer secondary (as is the case today), builders in these earlier times would have been faced with the uninviting prospect of obtaining expensive vacuum tubes and providing for their mechanical and electrical needs. Think about it. A single solid-state rectifier (tiny in size) replaces a large vacuum tube, the filament supply for the tube, the mounting socket, and much more. From a mechanical standpoint alone, the vacuum tube rectifier consisted of a minimum of four connections and required chassis cutting, socket mounting with nuts and bolts, and a number of other steps for completion. Remember, too, that it was necessary to supply an operating potential for the vacuum tube filaments. Today, the solid-state rectifier is simply soldered to the circuit at two points and is self-operating, requiring no internal supply. When compared with vacuum tube rectifier installations, this is a tremendous savings in parts and time.

Solid-state diodes may also be used in simple, self-driven modulator circuits, as frequency multipliers, as frequency modulators, and for low-voltage switching functions. Zener diodes can replace an expensive bank of gaseous regulator tubes and do so in a scant fraction of the physical space required for the latter. For high-voltage and/or high-current applications, diodes may be wired in series or in parallel. This allows inexpensive single components to be used in circuits that would require costly devices if single-component design were mandatory.

From a power switching standpoint, the silicon-controlled rectifier (for direct-current applications) and the triac (for alternating current) offer almost limitless control in a single package. A few decades ago, sophisticated electronic circuits consisting of vacuum tubes and all the many components that allowed them to operate would have been necessary. The remarkable thing about solid-state diodes of all types lies in the fact that they perform their electronic functions with less expense, less installation time, and far less space requirements and often do so much more efficiently than their vacuum tube counterparts.

All these attributes make the solid-state diode in all its many configurations one of the most valuable tools of the electronics industry. I could make similar comparisons between transistors and vacuum tubes and even between integrated circuits and transistors, but the point here is that each type of component is revolutionary and each deserves its own position of equal importance. The solid-state diode, however, has become so ingrained in the electronics industry and in the minds of electronic experimenters that it is often thought of as insignificant when compared with other solid-state components.

Robert J. Traister

The Experimenter's Guide
to Solid-State Diodes

Semiconductor
Junctions

In the study of electronics, the association of matter and electricity is of paramount importance. Since every electronic device is constructed of parts made from ordinary matter, the effects of electricity on matter must be well understood. As a means of accomplishing this, all the elements of which matter is made may be placed in one of three categories: conductors, semiconductors, and insulators. Conductors, for example, are elements such as copper and silver which will conduct a flow of electricity very readily. Due to their good conducting abilities, they are formed into wire and used whenever it is desired to transfer electrical energy from one point to another. Insulators (nonconductors), on the other hand, do not conduct electricity to any great degree and are therefore used when it is desirable to prevent a flow of electricity. Substances such as sulfur, rubber, and glass are good insulators. Materials such as germanium and silicon are not good conductors in the natural state. However, when they are treated with certain impurities they take on properties that lie somewhere between a conductor and an insulator. These specially treated in-between materials are then classified as semiconductors. The term semi-resistors would probably be just as appropriate, but the former is always used to describe them.

The electrical conductivity of matter is ultimately dependent on the energy levels of the atoms of which the material is constructed. In any solid material, such as copper, the atoms which make up the molecular structure are bound together in the lattice. Since the atoms of copper are firmly fixed in position within the lattice structure, they are not free to migrate through the material and therefore cannot carry the electricity through the conductor without application of external forces.

In the pure form, semiconductor materials are of little use in electronics. When a certain amount of impurity is added, however, the material will have more (or less) free electrons than holes, depending on the kind of impurity added. Both forms of conduction will be present, but the *majority carrier* will be dominant. The holes are called positive carriers, and the electrons are called negative carriers. The one present in the greatest quantity is called the majority carrier; the other is called the minority carrier. The quality and quantity of the impurity are carefully controlled by a process known as doping. The added impurities will create either an excess or a deficiency of electrons, depending on the kind of impurity added.

The impurities that are important in semiconductor materials are those that align themselves in the regular lattice structure, whether they have one valence electron too many or one valence electron too few. The first type loses its extra electron easily, and in so doing, increases the conductivity of the material by contributing a free electron. This type of impurity has five valence electrons and is called a pentavalent impurity. Arsenic, antimony, bismuth, and phosphorus are pentavalent impurities. Because these materials give up or donate one electron to the material, they are called donor impurities.

The second type of impurity tends to compensate for its deficiency of one valence electron by acquiring an electron from its neighbor. Impurities of this type in the lattice structure have only three electrons and are called trivalent impurities. Aluminum, indium, gallium, and boron are trivalent impurities. Because these materials accept one electron from the material, they are called acceptor impurities.

N-TYPE GERMANIUM

When a pentavalent (donor) impurity like arsenic is added to germanium, it will form covalent bonds with the germanium atoms. Figure 1-1 illustrates an arsenic atom (As) in a germanium lattice structure. The arsenic atom has five valence electrons in its outer shell but uses only four of them to form covalent bonds with the germanium atoms, leaving one electron relatively free in the crystal structure. Because this type of material conducts by electron movement, it is called a negative-carrier type of N-type semicon-

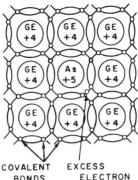

FIGURE 1-1 Germanium lattice with
donor impurity added.

COVALENT   EXCESS
BONDS   ELECTRON

ductor. Pure germanium may be converted into an *N*-type semiconductor by doping it with a donor impurity consisting of any element containing five electrons in its outer shell. The amount of the impurity added is very small; it is on the order of one atom of impurity in 10 million atoms of germanium.

P-TYPE GERMANIUM

A trivalent (acceptor) impurity element can also be added to pure germanium to dope the material. In this case, the impurity has one less electron than it needs to establish covalent bonds with four neighboring atoms. Thus, in one covalent bond, there will be only one electron instead of two. This arrangement leaves a hole in that covalent bond.

Figure 1-2 shows the germanium lattice structure with the addition of an indium atom (In). The indium atom has one electron less than it needs to form covalent bonds with the four neighboring atoms and thus creates a hole in the structure. Gallium and boron also exhibit these characteristics. The holes are present only if a

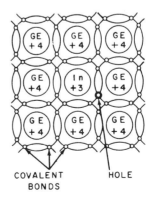

FIGURE 1-2 Germanium lattice with
acceptor impurity added.

COVALENT   HOLE
BONDS

P-Type Germanium   **3**

trivalent impurity is used. Note that a hole carrier is not created by the removal of an electron from a neutral atom but is created when a trivalent impurity enters into covalent bonds with a tetravalent (four valence electrons) crystal structure. Because this semiconductor material conducts by the movement of holes which are positive charges, it is called a positive-carrier-type or P-type semiconductor. When an electron fills a hole (Fig. 1-3), the hole appears to move to the spot previously occupied by the electron.

When a donor material such as arsenic is added to germanium, the fifth electron in the outer ring of the arsenic atom does not become a part of a covalent bond. This extra electron (when acted on by some force) may move away from the arsenic atom to one of the nearby germanium atoms in the N-type material.

The arsenic atom has a positive charge of five units on the inner circle, as shown in Fig. 1-1, and when the electron moves away from the arsenic atom, there will be only four electrons to neutralize the positive charge. As a result, there will be a region of positive charge around the arsenic atom. Similarly, the excess electron that has moved into the germanium atom outer shell makes a total of five electrons instead of four for that atom of germanium. Thus, there is a region of negative charge around this atom.

Although there is a region of positive charge around the arsenic atom after the electron has moved away and a region of negative charge around the germanium atom with the extra electron, the total charge on the N-type crystal remains the same. In other words, the total charge is zero. There are exactly enough electrons to neutralize the positive charges on the nuclei of all the atoms in the crystal. However, because some of the electrons may move about in the crystal, there will be regions in the crystal where there are negative charges and other regions where there will be positive charges, even though the net charge on the crystal is zero.

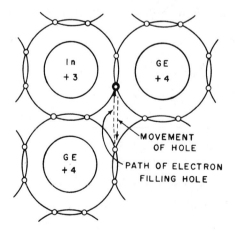

MOVEMENT OF HOLE

PATH OF ELECTRON FILLING HOLE

FIGURE 1-3 Hole movement within a germanium lattice.

In a *P*-type material having an impurity such as indium added to it, a similar situation may exist. Indium has only three electrons in its outer ring. Three electrons are all that are needed to neutralize the net positive charge of three units on the inner circle (Fig. 1-2). However, with only three electrons in the outer shell, there is a hole in one of the covalent bonds formed between the indium atom and the four adjacent germanium atoms. If an electron moves in to fill this hole (Fig. 1-3), there is one more electron in the indium atom than is needed to neutralize the positive charge of three units. Thus, there will be a region of negative charge around the indium atom.

Similarly, if one of the germanium atoms gives up an electron to fill the hole in the covalent bond, the germanium atom will be short an electron, and there will be a region of positive charge around this atom. While the giving up of an electron by a germanium atom plus the acquisition of an electron by the indium atom charges (ionizes) both atoms involved, the net charge on the *P*-type crystal is still zero. There is one atom that is short an electron and another atom that has one too many. The crystal itself does not acquire any charge.

These ionized atoms produced in both *N*- and *P*-type germanium are not concentrated in any one part of the crystal but instead are spread uniformly throughout the crystal. If any region within the crystal were to have a very large number of positively charged atoms, these atoms would attract free electrons from other parts of the crystal to neutralize part of the charged atoms so that the charge would spread uniformly through the crystal. Similarly, if a large number of atoms within a small region had an excess of electrons, these electrons would repel each other and spread through the crystal.

As stated previously, both holes and electrons are involved in conduction. In *N*-type material, the electrons are the majority carriers, and the holes are the minority carriers. In *P*-type material, the holes are the majority carriers, and the electrons are the minority carriers.

CURRENT FLOW IN *N*-TYPE MATERIAL

Current flow through an *N*-type material is illustrated in Fig. 1-4. Conduction in this type of semiconductor is similar to the conduction in a copper conductor. That is, the application of voltage across the material will cause the loosely bound electron to be released from the impurity atom, and it will move toward the positive potential point.

Certain differences do exist, however, between the *N*-type semiconductor and a copper conductor. For example, the semiconductor resistance decreases with temperature increase, because more carriers

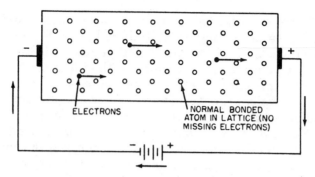

FIGURE 1-4 Current flow in *N*-type semiconductor material.

are made available at higher temperatures. Increasing the temperature releases electrons from more of the impurity atoms in the lattice,
causing increased conductivity (decreased resistance). In the copper
conductor, increasing the temperature does not increase the number
of carriers but increases the thermal agitation or vibration of the structure so as to impede the current flow further (increase the resistance).

CURRENT FLOW IN *P*-TYPE MATERIAL

Current flow through a *P*-type material is illustrated in Fig. 1-5.
Conduction in this material is by positive carriers (holes) from the
positive to the negative terminal. Electrons from the negative terminal cancel holes in the vicinity of the terminal, while at the
positive terminal, electrons are being removed from the covalent
bonds, thus creating new holes. The new holes then move toward

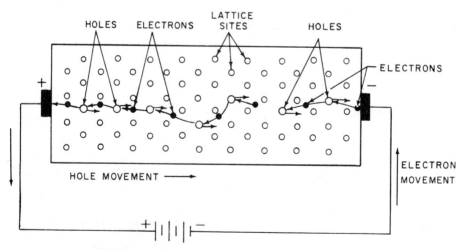

FIGURE 1-5 Current flow in *P*-type semiconductor material.

6 Semiconductor Junctions

the negative terminal (the electrons shifting to the positive terminal) and are canceled by more electrons emitted from the negative terminal. This process continues as a steady stream of holes (hole current) moving toward the negative terminal.

In both N- and P-type materials, current flow in the external circuit is out of the negative terminal of the battery and into the positive terminal.

PN JUNCTIONS

Elements whose atoms contain four valence electrons are classified as semiconductors. Examples of such elements are germanium and silicon. These semiconductor materials are of little use in electronics in their pure or intrinsic form. However, when they are tainted or doped with a small amount of impurity material, they form the basis for a myriad of solid-state electronic devices. The impurity elements, added to semiconductor materials, fall into one of two categories: pentavalent, those with five valence electrons, and trivalent, those with three valence electrons. When a pentavalent impurity is added to a semiconductor material, the result is called N-type material. When a trivalent impurity is added, P-type material is formed.

Both N- and P-type semiconductor materials are electrically neutral. However, a block of intrinsic semiconductor material may be doped with pentavalent and trivalent impurities so as to make half the crystal N material and the other half P material. A force will then exist across the junction of the N and P material. The force is an electro-chemical attraction by the P material for electrons in the N material. This force exists because the trivalent impurity has caused a deficiency of electrons within the structure of the P material, while the pentavalent impurity has caused an excess of electrons within the structure of the N material.

Due to the above-mentioned force, electrons will be caused to leave the N material and enter the P material. This will make the N material in proximity to the junction positive with respect to the remainder of the N material. Also, the P material in proximity to the junction will become negative with respect to the remaining P material. This is illustrated in Fig. 1-6.

After the initial movement of charges, further migration of electrons ceases due to the equalization of electron concentration in the immediate vicinity of the junction. The charged areas on either side of the junction constitute a potential barrier, or junction barrier, which prevents further current flow. This region is also called a depletion region.

Several facts must be emphasized. The junction barrier exists

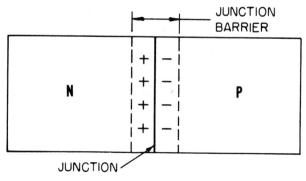

FIGURE 1-6 *PN* junction.

only for a minute distance on either side of the junction. The formation of a barrier occurs only in a homogeneous crystal which has been properly doped. That is, doping two separate sections of crystal and then placing them in contact will not produce the desired phenomenon. Finally, the barrier is formed at the instant the crystal is manufactured, and the magnitude of the barrier is a function of the particular crystal.

The device described above is a semiconductor junction diode. The schematic symbol for a semiconductor diode is illustrated in Fig. 1-7. This device allows appreciable current flow in one direction while restricting current flow to an almost negligible value in the other direction. The *N*-material section of the device is called the cathode, and the *P*-material section is called the anode. The device permits current flow from cathode to anode and restricts current flow from anode to cathode. This action will be described further.

Consider the case wherein a potential is placed externally across the diode positive on the anode with respect to the cathode. This is depicted in Fig. 1-8. The applied voltage, called bias, is in opposition to the junction barrier potential. If this voltage is increased from zero, the junction barrier will be progressively reduced, and current flow through the device will increase. This is depicted in Fig. 1-9. Eventually, the barrier will be eliminated, and current flow will increase rapidly with an increase in voltage. This polarity of voltage

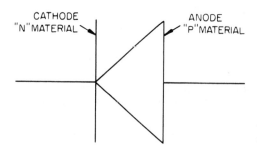

FIGURE 1-7 **Schematic representation of a *PN* junction diode indicating cathode and anode materials.**

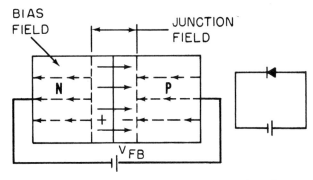

FIGURE 1-8 *PN* junction diode in the forward-biased state.

(anode positive with respect to the cathode) is called forward bias, since it causes the device to conduct an appreciable current flow.

Next, consider the case wherein the anode is made negative with respect to the cathode. Figure 1-10 illustrates this reverse bias condition. Note that the reverse bias voltage aids the junction barrier potential. In effect, the barrier is increased. This is depicted in Fig. 1-11. It would seem that no current flow should be possible under this reverse bias condition. However, since the block of semiconductor material is not a perfect insulator, a very small reverse or leakage current will flow. At normal operating temperatures, this current may be neglected. It is noteworthy, however, that leakage current increases with an increase in temperature.

Figure 1-12 is a graph of the current flow through a semiconductor diode, plotted by values of anode to cathode voltage. Note that the forward current increases slowly at low values of forward bias. As the forward bias is increased, the barrier is neutralized, and current increases rapidly for further increases in applied voltage. It should be noted that excessive forward bias could destroy the device through excessive forward current.

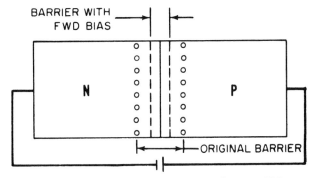

FIGURE 1-9 Effective forward bias on barrier width.

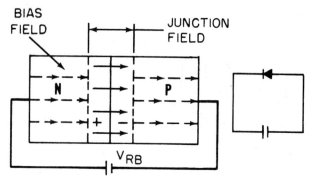

FIGURE 1-10 Reverse-biased *PN* junction.

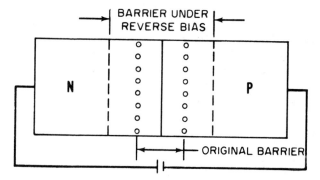

FIGURE 1-11 During the reverse-biased mode, barrier width increases.

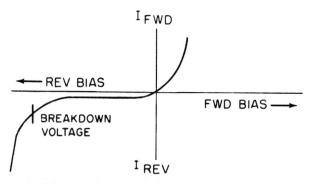

FIGURE 1-12 Semiconductor diode characteristic curve.

With reverse bias applied, a very small reverse current exists. This reverse current increases minutely, with an increase in reverse current. However, if an excessive reverse voltage is applied, the structure of the semiconductor material may be broken down by the resulting high electric stress, and the device may be terminated. The value of reverse voltage at which this breakdown occurs is called the avalanche or breakdown voltage. At this voltage, current increases rapidly with small increases in reverse bias. This region of rapidly increasing current flow is called the avalanche region. Certain semiconductor devices are designed and doped to operate in the avalanche region without harm.

2

Diode
Specifications

Semiconductor materials treated to form *PN* junctions are used extensively in electronic circuitry. Variations in doping agent concentrations and physical size of the substrate produce diodes which are suited for different applications. There are signal diodes, rectifiers, zener diodes, reference diodes, varactors, and others.

Pictorial representations of various diodes are shown in Fig. 2-1. This is but a very limited representation of the wide assortment in case design. However, the shape of characteristic curves of these diodes is very similar; primarily, current and voltage limits and relationships are different. Figure 2-2 shows a typical curve of a junction diode. The graph shows two different kinds of bias. Bias in the *PN* junction is the difference in potential between the anode (*P* material) and the cathode (*N* material). Forward bias is the application of a voltage between *N* and *P* material, where the *P* material is positive with respect to the *N* material. When the *P* material becomes negative with respect to the *N* material, the junction is reverse biased. Application of greater and greater amounts of forward bias causes more and more forward current until the power-handling capability of the diode is exceeded, unless limited by external circuitry. Small amounts of forward bias cause very little current flow until the internal barrier potential is overcome. The potential difference varies from diode to diode but is usually no more

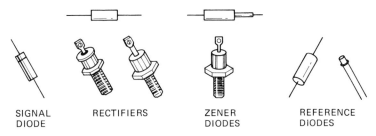

SIGNAL DIODE RECTIFIERS ZENER DIODES REFERENCE DIODES

FIGURE 2-1 Various types of junction diodes.

than a few tenths of a volt. Reverse bias produces a very small amount of reverse current until the breakdown point is reached; then an increase in reverse bias will cause a large increase in reverse current. Therefore, if breakdown is not exceeded, the ratio of forward current to reverse current is large, for example, milliamperes to microamperes or amperes to milliamperes. Changes in temperature may cause alterations in the characteristic curve, such as slope of curve at any point, breakdown point, amount of reverse current, etc.

There are many specifications listed in various manufacturers' technical sheets and in semiconductor data manuals. Descriptions of various types and their more important electrical characteristics follow.

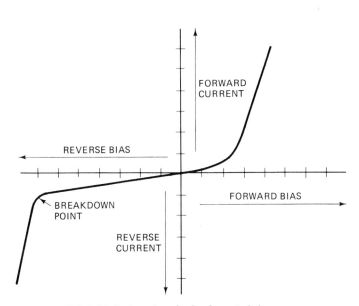

FIGURE 2-2 Junction diode characteristic curve.

RECTIFIER DIODES

Rectifier diodes are used primarily in power supplies. These diodes are usually of the silicon type because of this material's inherent reliability and higher overall performance compared to other materials. Silicon allows higher forward conductance, lower reverse leakage current, and operation at higher temperatures compared to other materials.

The major electrical characteristics of rectifier diodes are the following:

dc blocking voltage (V_R): maximum reverse dc voltage which will not cause breakdown.

Average forward voltage drop (V_F): average forward voltage drop across the rectifier given at a specified forward current and temperature, usually specified for rectified forward current at 60 Hz.

Average rectifier forward current (I_0): average rectified forward current at a specified temperature, usually at 60 Hz with a resistive load. The temperature is normally specified for a range, typically −65 to +174°C.

Average reverse current (I_R): average reverse current at a specified temperature, usually at 60 Hz.

Peak surge current (I_{SURGE}): peak current specified for a given number of cycles or portion of a cycle, for example, $\frac{1}{2}$ cycle at 60 Hz.

SIGNAL DIODES

Signal diodes fall into various categories, such as general purpose, high-speed switch, parametric amplifiers, etc. These devices are used as mixers, detectors, and switches as well as in many other applications.

Signal diodes' major electrical characteristics are as follows:

Peak reverse voltage (PRV): maximum reverse voltage which can be applied before reaching the breakdown point.

Reverse current (I_R): small value of direct current that flows when a semiconductor diode has reverse bias.

Maximum forward voltage drop at indicated forward current $(V_F @ L_F)$: maximum forward voltage drop across the diode at the indicated forward current.

Reverse recovery time (t_{rr}): time required for reverse current to decrease from a value equal to the forward current to a value equal to I_R when a step function of voltage is applied.

CATHODE (N-TYPE) ANODE (P-TYPE)

FORWARD CURRENT

FIGURE 2-3 Schematic diagram for a diode rectifier.

The schematic diagram for the rectifier and signal diode is shown in Fig. 2-3. Forward current flows into the point of the arrow, and reverse current is with the arrow.

ZENER DIODES

The zener diode is unique compared to other diodes in that it is designed to operate reverse biased in the avalanche or breakdown region. The device is used as a regulator, clipper, and coupling device and in other applications.

The major electrical characteristics of zener diodes are the following:

Nominal zener breakdown $(V_{Z(NOM)})$: sometimes a $V_{Z(MAX)}$ and $V_{Z(MIN)}$ are used to set absolute limits between which breakdown will occur.

Maximum power dissipation (P_D): maximum power the device is capable of handling. Since voltage is a constant, there is a corresponding current maximum (I_{ZM}).

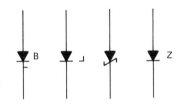

FIGURE 2-4 Zener diode schematic symbols.

Schematic diagrams of the zener are shown in Fig. 2-4. Zener current flows in the direction of the arrow. In many schematics, a distinction is not made for this diode, and a signal diode symbol is used.

REFERENCE DIODES

Reference diodes were developed to replace zener diodes in certain applications because of the zener's temperature instability. Reference diodes provide a constant voltage over a wide temperature range. The important characteristic of this device, besides V_Z, is T_{MIN}.

T_{MAX}, which specifies the range over which an indicated temperature coefficient is applicable. The temperature coefficient is expressed as a percent of reference (V_Z) per degree centigrade change in temperature.

VARACTOR DIODES

PN junctions exhibit capacitance properties because the depletion area represents a dielectric and the adjacent semiconductor material represents two conductive plates. Increasing reverse bias decreases this capacitance, while increasing forward bias increases it. When forward bias is large enough to overcome the barrier potential, high forward conduction destroys the capacitance effect, except at very high frequencies. Therefore, the effective capacitance is a function of external applied voltage. This characteristic is undesirable in conventional diode operation but is enhanced by special doping in the varactor or variable-capacitance (varicap) diodes. Application categories of the varactor can be divided into two main types: tuning and harmonic generation. Different characteristics are required by the two types, but both use the voltage-dependent junction capacitance effect. Figure 2-5 shows the voltage-capacitance relationships. The use of this diode for frequency multiplication (harmonic generation) is common.

As a variable capacitor, the varactor is rugged and small, is not affected by dust or moisture, and is ideal for remote control and precision fine tuning. The current uses of tuning diodes span the spectrum from AM radio to the microwave region. The most significant parameters of a tuning diode are the capacitance ratio Q, series resistance, nominal capacitance, leakage current, and breakdown voltage.

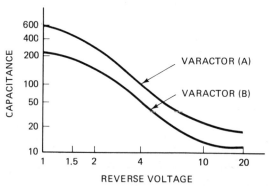

FIGURE 2-5 Typical voltage-capacitance relationship in varactor diodes.

The capacitance ratio, which defines the tuning range, is the amount of capacitance variation over the bias voltage range. It is normally expressed as the ratio of the low-voltage capacitance divided by the high-voltage capacitance. For example, a typical specification which reads $C_4/C_{60} = 3$ indicates that the capacitance value at 4V is 3 times the capacitance value at 60 V. The high voltage in the ratio is usually the minimum breakdown voltage specification. A 4-V lower limit is quite common, since it describes the approximate lower limit of linear operation for most devices. The capacitance ratio of tuning diodes varies in accordance with construction.

Q is inversely proportional to frequency, nominal capacitance, and series resistance. Ideally, tuning diodes should have high Q, low series resistance, low reverse leakage, and high breakdown voltage at any desired capacitance ratio. However, as might be expected, these parameters are not unrelated, and improving one degrades another, so that often a compromise must be reached. As a rule, diodes with low capacitance values have the highest Q.

Various schematic symbols are used to designate varactor diodes, as shown in Fig. 2-6. The application of the varactor as a control device in LC tanks will be described. The resonant frequency of any tank circuit containing L and C is found by the formula $F_r = \frac{1}{2}\pi\sqrt{LC}$. By changing the values of either L or C, we change the resonant frequency of the tank. The resonant frequency of a tank can be changed mechanically (i.e., the use of a movable slug in the coil or the movement of plates on a variable capacitor). However, the varactor provides a means of obtaining electronic control of the tuned tank.

Capacitors in parallel add so as to give an increased capacitance value. If one of the capacitors is variable, the range of the combination is also variable. Figure 2-7 shows a varactor that is controlled by a variable voltage supply; the junction capacitance of the device is part of the tank's reactive components. The degree of reverse bias across the varactor will determine the capacitance of the varactor. C_2 blocks dc current flow through L_1. As the varactor's capacitance is varied, the resonant frequency of the tuned tank composed of L_1, C_1, and the junction capacitance will change. If C_2 is large in comparison to the junction capacitance, C_2 will have a minimal effect in determining the resonant frequency. A decrease in the re-

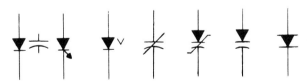

FIGURE 2-6   Varactor diode schematic symbols.

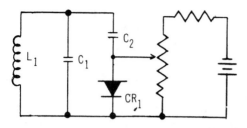

FIGURE 2-7 Using a varactor diode to alter resonant frequency.

verse bias on the varactor will cause an increase in its capacitance. The increase in capacitance causes the overall capacitance (C_1 and varactor) to increase, with a resultant decrease in resonant frequency of the circuit. An increase in reverse bias of the diode causes an opposite effect on resonant frequency.

PHYSICAL SPECIFICATIONS

Common *PN* junction diodes and rectifiers may be packaged in many different ways. The most common arrangement is shown in Fig. 2-8. Here, the semiconductor junction is contained in a canister or tube which is commonly $\frac{1}{3}$ in. long and possesses axial leads. Often, the diode schematic symbol is imprinted on the package case, which indicates the anode and cathode leads. Alternately, a small band may encircle one end of the case, indicating the cathode lead only. Sometimes the package will be a bullet-shaped cylinder, as shown in Fig. 2-9. Again, a band or schematic symbol may be used to indicate the cathode and anode, but where these are not present, the sloped portion of the case is usually the cathode side of the device.

Figure 2-10 shows another method of packaging. Here, the axial leads are done away with and are replaced with metallic connectors which are designed for snap-in friction connections with an appropriate receptacle. Diodes may also be seen in packages which contain radial leads. Some examples are shown in Fig. 2-11. Many of these devices look very much like transistors, with the exception that the diodes contain two leads, while transistors will contain three or more. Exact replacement diodes from one manufacturer may be packaged differently from those of another. The two may be electronically identical, but the physical packaging may lead to some installation problems when one type differs greatly from another.

FIGURE 2-8. Circular can diode package.

FIGURE 2-9 Bullet-shaped diode package.

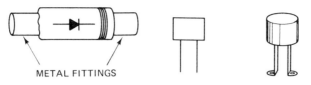

FIGURE 2-10 Diode packaging for snap-in fitting.

FIGURE 2-11 Diodes with radial leads.

High-current diodes may require external heat sink installation and are therefore packaged quite differently from those components which are designed to pass a forward current of 3 A or less. Figure 2-12 shows a typical high-current diode which may be rated at 10, 15, 20, or more amperes of forward current. The case is made from metal and is fitted with a threaded anode connection which is inserted through the appropriate opening in the heat sink and then secured by means of a lock washer and mating nut. These devices may be used without a heat sink but at tremendously reduced current levels. The large, metallic cases which are typical of such high-current devices are designed to dissipate heat directly into the heat sink and are far larger than the moderate- to low-current devices discussed earlier.

Diodes which contain specialized cases are often given more or less universal package numbers. Figure 2-13 shows two types of packages. One is designated as a DO-4 type, while the other is a DO-5. The physical dimensions of each type of case are provided in these drawings. Note that the DO-4 contains a longer threaded shaft and is more narrow in width when compared with the DO-5, which exhibits a shorter anode shaft. Generally speaking, the forward current rating of the diode will determine the physical size of the case, with the larger cases containing the higher-rated components.

Diode packages serve two basic functions. First, they protect the delicate *PN* junction from direct mechanical shocks which could easily break it. Second and equally as important, the case draws heat

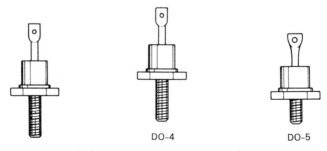

DO-4   DO-5

FIGURE 2-12 Power diode.

FIGURE 2-13 Example of two power diode packages.

away from the junction. As current passes through the *PN* junction, a certain amount of heat is created due to internal resistance. This is called the I^2R loss and is directly dependent on the internal resistance and the amount of forward current. Operating voltage has nothing to do with this heat buildup. For this reason, a diode which is conducting a forward current of 1 A at 12 V dc will give off as much heat as one with a forward current of 1A at 1200 V dc, assuming the same internal resistance in both examples. The anode lead is normally connected directly to the metallic case. Since the case has a larger surface area than the *PN* junction, heat is drawn to the larger body. Devices which do not require external heat sinks have cases which are adequate to keep the *PN* junction within safe temperature limits and depend on the ability of the case to get rid of heat into the surrounding air. Devices which do require heat sinks depend on the ability of the larger case to conduct heat to the heat sink, which actually becomes part of the device case. The heat sink contains a relatively large surface area (in relationship to the case and the junction) and, in turn, dissipates heat into the air. A thorough discussion on heat sinks and mounting techniques is provided in Chapter 3.

PACKAGED RECTIFIERS

In recent years, specialized rectifier circuits have been offered in single packages. For example, a bridge rectifier normally requires the connection of four single rectifiers, but in a bridge package, all these discrete components are housed in one small container. A bridge rectifier package is shown in Fig. 2-14 and contains four leads. Two of these are to be connected to the ac output of a power transformer, while the remaining two provide a positive and negative rectified output. Normally, the ac connections are labeled "ac." Alternately, a sine-wave designation (~) will be used. The dc output terminals are typically marked with a plus (+) and minus (−) sign indicating the polarity.

While bridge rectifier packages are common, some are also set up for full-wave center-tapped configurations. Specialized packages for television receivers may also contain complete voltage tripler or quadrupler circuits in one unit. Device packaging of this type serves to conserve space during the assembly process. For example, when

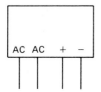
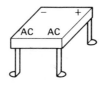

FIGURE 2-14 Solid-state rectifier assembly.

building a full-wave bridge circuit using discrete components, it is necessary to mount four diodes on a piece of circuit board and to solder the interconnecting wiring. This takes up a relatively large amount of space. When a bridge rectifier package is used, the total space consumed in the single package is greatly reduced, since the dimensions of the latter device are usually about 1 in. square and a $\frac{1}{2}$ in. in depth, not including leads. The use of packages, then, does away with the circuit board and requires only that the four leads be soldered to the transformer output and dc output, respectively.

Packaged rectifier circuits are usually not available in high-current designs. Maximum ratings are normally held to within 3 A of forward current and a maximum peak inverse voltage rating of 1000 V. Higher peak inverse voltage (PIV) ratings can sometimes be obtained by using another type of packaged circuit. We shall learn later in this chapter how diodes may be combined in series to increase this rating; but again, this requires the interconnection of several discrete components. When this is done in a rectifier package, the circuit board is again done away with, and a compact circuit is housed in one unit. High-voltage rectifier packages normally combine three or four 1000-PIV diodes in a series connection which yields a total PIV rating of 3000 or 4000 V. These units are simply treated as a single rectifier with a high PIV rating and are combined to form bridge circuits, voltage doublers, etc. In both cases, more than one packaged diode will be required, but the overall result is a much smaller completed circuit in regard to physical size.

RECTIFIER COMBINATORIAL RATINGS

A rectifier is a device which will conduct current in one direction but not in the other. For this reason, these devices are used mainly to convert alternating current into direct current. The two ratings which we are most concerned with when using diodes for rectification purposes are peak inverse voltage (PIV), often referred to as peak reverse voltage (PRV), and forward current (I_0). The peak inverse voltage rating determines the potential which a device is capable of withstanding during the nonconducting state, while the forward current rating indicates the amount of average current the device can safely conduct.

To explain the rectification operation, imagine an alternating-current waveform such as the one shown in Fig. 2-15. It can be seen here that the current swings from a zero value to a peak positive value, then passes through a zero value again, and advances to a peak negative value. Standard house current in the United States completes one of these cycles in $\frac{1}{60}$ s. Sixty such cycles are completed

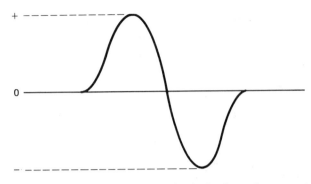

FIGURE 2-15 Graphic representation of a single alternating-current cycle.

every second. Thus, standard house current has a frequency of 60 H, a hertz being one complete cycle in 1 s.

When the ac output is connected to a rectifier circuit, conduction will occur only during one phase of the cycle (either positive or negative depending on the rectifier configuration). Assuming that the rectifier is set up to conduct during the positive cycle only, the positive portion of the original ac input waveform will be allowed to pass. The negative portion of the cycle will not be conducted, as it is effectively blocked by the rectifier. The graphic output of such a rectifier circuit is shown in Fig. 2-16. The nonconductive portion of the original ac waveform is shown by the dotted line in the negative portion of the graph. It should be pointed out that this graph is used to illustrate voltage potentials only, especially as they apply to the PIV rating. Assuming that the peak voltage level in the graph is 150, then the rectifier used must have a PIV rating of at least 150 V so that it will not be damaged during the nonconducting state. Put simply, during this state, the current at the 150-V potential is trying to pass through the rectifier, but the device is blocking this flow. If the rectifier is not sufficiently rated, then current at the 150-V potential can indeed break through and destroy the device. Again, this is a simplis-

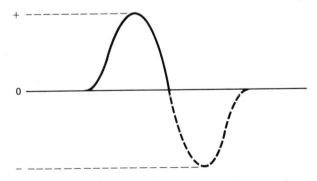

FIGURE 2-16 Effective rectification upon previous waveform.

tic explanation and may not stand up under a close theoretical inspection.

This book is written from a practical standpoint and is designed for the individual who wishes to learn about diodes and actually construct projects using commonly available components. A book which includes projects that require highly specialized components may be next to useless to the average builder who pursues electronics as a hobby. For example, high-voltage rectifier packages rated at 9000 PIV or more are available from industrial suppliers, but these can be quite costly, especially when purchased in quantities of 2 or 3 rather than 100 or more. Indeed, some projects in this book may require this type of rating, but fortunately there is an inexpensive way to obtain these values using a number of discrete components. When doing this, a thorough knowledge of combinatorial ratings is mandatory.

Silicon rectifiers may be purchased from local electronics hobby stores and surplus suppliers for less than 25 cents each. About the highest ratings you will find here, however, are 1000 PIV at 1 to 3 A. Assume that you need a rectifier with a forward current rating of 1 A and a PIV of 4000 V dc. First, the 1-A rating of one of these inexpensive diodes is adequate, but the PIV rating falls short. You can purchase a 3000-PIV packaged rectifier for $12 to $15, but you can also build one from three of these cheap diodes for less than $2.

Figure 2-17 shows a basic schematic diagram for a rectifier circuit that will yield an effective overall rating of 3000 PIV at 1 A. This is a series connection of the three components. In such a circuit, the PIV ratings of the diodes multiply (by the total number of diodes in the circuit), while the current rating remains identical to that of a single diode. Therefore, three 1000-PIV 1-A diodes in a series circuit yield the equivalent of a 3000-PIV 1-A single-unit rectifier.

The circuit shown is not generally usable directly due to another specification which has not been previously mentioned. All solid-state rectifiers and diodes have a certain internal resistance. This is a very small ohmic value and is typically .8 Ω (approximately) in 1000-PIV 1-A units. However, the resistance can vary from component to component, even if all are rated identically and are made by the same manufacturer. This presents no problem in most rectifier hookups,

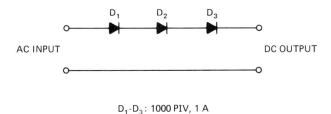

D_1-D_3: 1000 PIV, 1 A

FIGURE 2-17   Series-connected rectifiers for PIV increase.

Rectifier Combinatorial Ratings   23

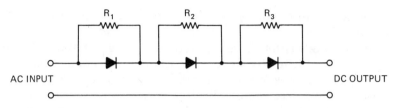

R₁-R₃: EQUALIZING RESISTORS

FIGURE 2-18 Parallel equalization resistors are used to minimize internal differences in series diode strings.

but when combining units in series, small differences can allow the components with fractionally lower internal resistance specifications to assume more than their fair share of circuit voltage. In the previous example, each rectifier should drop a maximum of 1000 V. However, if one exhibited a slightly lower resistance than the other two, this particular component might drop 1500 V while the other two dropped only 750 each. This would mean that one diode would be subjected to more than 1000 PIV, which is in excess of its rating.

To overcome this factor, equalizing resistors are normally used in series rectifier configurations. This is shown in Fig. 2-18. Here, three resistors have been wired in parallel with the diodes. The resistance value is not critical but should be very high. Most designers today will use 470-kΩ $\frac{1}{2}$-W carbon resistors for similar applications. The high parallel resistance serves to equalize the internal resistances of the three diodes, allowing them each to drop one-third of the total circuit voltage. This prevents component burnout. Most series diode configurations will also contain an .01-μF 1000-V disk ceramic capacitor in parallel with each rectifier to prevent damage from voltage spikes which can occur when the circuit is initially activated.

While this discussion is applied to standard silicon rectifiers, it holds true for all types of diodes that will be discussed in later chapters. Detailed combinatorial ratings and circuit connection methods for silicon-controlled rectifiers, zener diodes, etc., will be provided in the chapters on these devices.

When it becomes necessary to use several diodes to increase the forward current rating of an individual unit, a parallel connection is required. This is shown in Fig. 2-19. Here, the effective yield from a

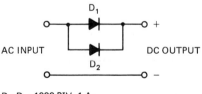

D₁-D₂: 1000 PIV, 1 A

FIGURE 2-19 Parallel connection of rectifiers for forward current increase.

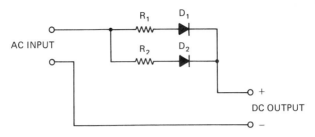

R₁-R₂: SERIES EQUALIZING RESISTORS

FIGURE 2-20 Series equalization resistors are often used to minimize internal differences in parallel-connected rectifiers.

circuit which uses two rectifiers, each rated at 1000 PIV and 1 A, will be 1000 PIV at 2 A. Note that in the parallel configuration the current rating of each diode is multiplied by the total number in the circuit. The PIV rating remains the same as that of an individual unit, regardless of the number of components used in the overall circuit. Here, internal resistance specifications also come into play. If the top diode has a slightly lower internal resistance rating than that of the second diode, then the former will pass more current and possibly exceed its rating. This problem is overcome by installing small-value series resistors in the circuit, as shown in Fig. 2-20. The value of these resistors will depend on the amount of current to be drawn from the circuit and may be anywhere from 5 to 100 Ω. Since each series resistor has a high value in relationship to the internal resistance of the rectifier, this effectively negates any differences between the two diodes.

It should be pointed out here that a parallel connection of diodes should be avoided whenever possible. In power supply circuits, especially those which draw higher amounts of current, the series resistors needed for device equalization can have an adverse effect on dynamic voltage regulation at the power supply output. Most complex connections of diodes today involve the previously discussed series connection, which induces little or no adverse operating effects to the overall circuit in which it is used.

A DISCUSSION IN PRACTICALITY

When building electronic circuits, reliability is of prime importance. Owing to this, the good builder usually opts for components which are rated substantially higher than the maximum circuit values anticipated. For example, if you were to design a circuit which would place a maximum theoretical peak inverse voltage on a rectifier of

100 V dc, then it would not be appropriate to choose a component with a maximum rating of 100 PIV. This is cutting it just too fine. First, you may have figured wrong, and, second, a surge in supply voltage or a minor circuit malfunction might conceivably increase the circuit PIV. Since a 1000-PIV rectifier is usually not appreciably more expensive than a 100-PIV unit, it would be practical to use one with the former rating. This would provide a safety margin of 10 times the normal expected inverse voltage. A 200-PIV unit would certainly be acceptable as well. When I build electronic circuits, I usually like to maintain at least a 50% safety margin. In other words, given the above example, I would choose a diode rated for at least 150 PIV. While this discussion has dealt with peak inverse voltage, the same safety criteria will apply to forward current, surge current, etc. With diodes, this is usually practical, but with some other electronic components, it may be necessary to settle for a safety margin of 10 to 20%. The projects contained in later chapters of this book specify components which have good safety margins regarding their stated specifications.

SUMMARY

Component ratings are used to indicate the maximum circuit parameters under which a device may be safely operated. Manufacturers often derate their components slightly in order to assure a higher degree of reliability, but this cannot always be counted on. For example, one manufacturer may produce a rectifier which is rated in specification sheets at 1000 PIV and 1 A. In fact, this component may have a true PIV rating closer to 1200 V and a forward current capability of 1.2 A. Another manufacturer may cut the tolerances far more closely. In any event, the stated maximum rating should always be considered as the true rating and must not be exceeded.

It is necessary to understand diode specifications in order to know how to choose the correct components for an electronic circuit. When circuits are designed from the ground up, circuit parameters must be figured ahead of time and components chosen solely based on these figures. It is also necessary to allow for an adequate safety margin of preferably 20% or more. This involves taking the theoretical circuit maximums and plussing them by 20%. The components are then chosen using the plussed ratings. This will assure a finished circuit which is able to operate properly over a varied range of conditions, some of which may involve higher values than were originally anticipated.

Owing to the increased ratings which may be had by combining two or more diodes in a series or parallel configuration, a great deal of savings can be had by using inexpensive, commonly available components. Cost is a major factor in any electronics pursuit, whether it be on an industrial or a hobby level. The resourceful builder must know how diodes may be combined and how to install the needed protective circuitry in order to produce circuits which are efficient electronically and economically.

3

Building
Techniques

It is one thing to know how to read schematic diagrams and another to build working circuits using them. I have met many persons who could theoretically discuss the circuits indicated by schematic diagrams in great detail but were completely helpless when it came to the actual construction process. The electronic builder must be well versed in both of these areas. This can only come with practice, although it is not absolutely essential to understand the in-depth theory of a particular circuit in order to successfully build it. Theory of operation, however, is most important when circuit alignment and/or troubleshooting become necessary.

There is nothing unusually difficult about building electronic circuits, especially those which are composed of solid-state components in addition to the usual assortment of capacitors, resistors, transformers, chokes, and other electrical-electronic devices. There are certain guidelines, however, which must be adhered to in order to arrive at a finished circuit which will not only work but will continue to work, often for many years.

The majority of home-built electronic circuits which fail to operate upon completion experiences this problem due to poor soldering technique. One or more solder connections are not made properly, so the circuit either refuses to operate at all or behaves in an erratic fashion. This has always been true, even in the days when solid-state components were unknown and vacuum tubes were used exclusively.

However, there may be a higher incidence of poorly soldered connections today due to the oft-spread general statement expounding upon the thermal vulnerability of semiconductor devices. Put simply, this statement indicates that diodes, transistors, and other solid-state devices can be quickly destroyed by high temperatures encountered even momentarily during the soldering process. In the vacuum tube days, wiring connections were made to tube sockets, so the devices themselves were not in the circuit during the soldering process. Then, too, vacuum tubes are not especially subject to thermal damage from the heat produced by a soldering iron or gun. While it is true that solid-state devices can be damaged by an improperly wielded soldering iron, I believe the possibilities of this have been blown far out of proportion. Certainly, this is a factor every builder will want to be aware of (thermal protection), but don't let it scare you to the point where solder connections are made hastily. For example, a builder is scared to death over the possibility of damaging an expensive solid-state component during the soldering process, so the soldering pencil is not left in contact with the joint long enough to properly bond it electrically. This is certainly a minor cause (and possibly a major one) of bad solder connections when dealing with solid-state components.

How sensitive are solid-state components to the heat from a soldering tool? I honestly don't have a full answer to that, but I can state definitely that it will depend on the component. Small signal diodes would certainly be more subject to thermal damage than would high-current rectifiers, for example. I did see a demonstration once where a metal-cased, small signal transistor was heated to a point where solder would melt on its case. It was then allowed to cool to normal temperature and then connected to an electronic circuit, where it worked perfectly. The trick, I was told, was in allowing the heated component to reach normal temperature again before operating current was applied. To make a long story short, I have only damaged one solid-state component due to thermal overheating in over 20 years of electronics building. This involved a small signal diode which was already connected at a terminal to which a copper conductor was also being attached. The bonding process took quite some time, and the glass-cased diode simply cracked and then broke in two pieces.

This discussion is by no means indicating that you should not pay any attention to possible thermal damage to solid-state devices and, indeed, other electronic components. The extent of heat required and the time period of its application in order to bring about damage are very difficult to define. The extent of damage is another factor. For example, a thermally damaged solid-state device may not work at all, may operate erratically, or may operate perfectly and then fail suddenly. In any event, there are certain procedures which will allow you to solder these devices to the other circuit elements without fear of damage. The moral here is to use the proper technique to thermally protect components while taking the proper amount of time to complete the solder joint. Don't be so frightened by rumors of instantaneous semiconductor destruction. Practice these rules, and your completed circuits should perform nicely.

SOLDERING TECHNIQUE

Soldering technique involves not only adherence to the step-by-step procedures involved but also having the appropriate tools to get the job done. The great majority of projects in this book will require a soldering pencil with a maximum rating of approximately 30 W. This provides an adequate amount of heat to make good, solid connections but will not produce a temperature which can easily damage any components. The ideal type of soldering iron is often called a soldering station. This is really a soldering pencil which contains a special circuit that regulates its temperature. In other words, the tip of the pencil will reach a certain maximum temperature which will then be maintained by the circuitry. Such a station is shown in Fig. 3-1. These are considerably more expensive than nonregulated soldering pencils. The latter sell for less then $10, while a soldering sta-

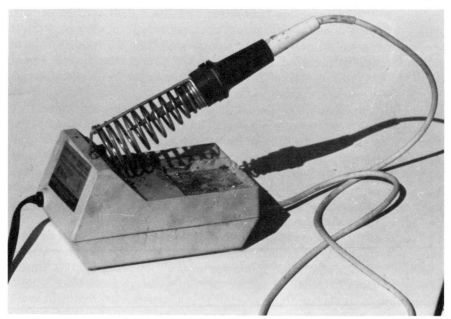

FIGURE 3-1 Temperature-regulated soldering station.

tion may cost $60 or more. If you plan to build a lot of electronic projects, the soldering station may be your best investment.

While there are many different types of solder, most can be lumped into one of two basic categories: acid core and resin core. The former is not suited for electronic work and must be avoided at all times. It contains a corrosive core which will quickly eat into circuit boards and component leads. This type is designed for the bonding of pipes and general plumbing applications.

Resin core solder is the kind sold by most electronics hobby stores and other similar outlets. It is designed to produce a good *electrical* bond when properly applied to a joint. A joint is formed when two component leads are wrapped together or around an electronic terminal strip, forming a good *mechanical* connection. It is prudent here to explain the differences between an electrical connection and a mechanical one. An electrical connection, bond, or joint is one which does not impede the flow of current. It may be very weak physically in that it can be pulled apart with the application of a small amount of pressure. The main purpose of an electrical connection is to allow for the unimpeded current flow between the components or circuits which are bonded together by the connection. A mechanical connection is one which is physically secure. It cannot be easily pried apart and is self-supporting and self-maintaining. A strong mechanical joint can be made by tying two pieces of string together in a secure knot. However, this would be a poor or nonexistent electrical connection. Here's the point: A strong mechanical connection is not necessarily a good electrical connection and vice versa.

Soldering a joint or connection provides only a good electrical bond. It does little in the way of adding mechanical strength. Put simply, two component leads must not be held together by solder alone. If this is done, the two elements may separate, breaking the electrical contact. It is mandatory that all solder joints be mechanically stable *before* solder is applied. This may mean simply wrapping two conductors together in pigtail fashion. This can also be accomplished by wrapping a single conductor around a metallic terminal and squeezing it tightly with a pair of pliers. Either way, gentle tugs on the two elements to be bonded should produce no movement within the joint itself. At this point, a good mechanical bond exists. Now solder may be applied to assure a good electrical bond.

The actual process of soldering is a fairly simple one but does require certain procedures to ensure a proper electrical bond. Before beginning, all elements of the solder joint must be clean. Often, grease or oil can build up on component leads. Dust and dirt can also hamper the bonding process. Generally, cleaning may be accomplished with a small strip of braided copper which acts as an abrasive. These soldering aids are sold in local electronics stores, but you may also pull the braid from a short piece of coaxial cable. The wire elements of the joint should normally be glossy. This indicates that all grease and possible oxide buildup have been removed. Once the wire elements and/or contact points have been cleaned, a good mechanical joint must be formed. This is done by tightly wrapping the elements so that no physical movement is possible.

It is at this point in the soldering process that many electronics project builders foul up. Too often, solder is simply heated with the iron and dropped onto the joint. This is completely wrong. As a matter of fact, the soldering iron should never touch the solder. The iron is applied to the joint itself, heating the elements until *they* are hot enough to melt the solder. In other words, the solder strip is held directly against the joint. If the elements have been heated to the proper temperature, the solder will flow throughout the joint. Apply enough solder to get the job done, but don't use too much. When excessive amounts of solder are applied, a cold solder joint is often formed. This does not provide a good electrical bond.

Once solder is flowing in the joint, remove the iron and allow about 10 s for cooling. During this period, make certain that the elements of the joint are not allowed to move in any way. If you have previously established a good mechanical bond, this should be no problem.

The joint should now be complete. By tugging on the wire elements, you can probably determine whether or not you have a good mechanical bond. A good electrical bond is indicated by examining the appearance of the soldered joint. It should be smooth and shiny. If the surface of the joint is rough and dull, this indicates a cold solder joint, and the process must be repeated.

The 10 s allowed for cooling of the joint once the solder has been applied should be more than adequate for any project in this book. However, in cases where very large contact surfaces must be soldered, an additional period of time for cooling may be needed. It is appropriate to mention one of the steps again. Do not apply the tip of the soldering iron to the solder itself. Rather, the soldering iron heats the wire elements of the joint, and these elements are the area to which the solder is applied. The joint, then, is heated to the same temperature as the soldering iron and literally pulls the molten solder throughout every recess.

THERMAL PROTECTION

While most types of solid-state devices may be soldered into electronic circuits by a low-wattage iron without fear of thermal damage, it's still a good idea to know how to protect these components. Sooner or later, you are bound to run into a situation where a low-wattage soldering tool is not available. When soldering guns which are not temperature regulated must be used, there is a possibility that component damage can occur, especially when a small diode or transistor must be attached to a large contact surface.

All you need to protect most types of components is some form of heat sink. A heat sink is any piece of metal which is large in relationship to the component lead. For small semiconductor devices, a small alligator clip will do nicely. Figure 3-2 shows how the clip is attached to the lead of a diode that is to be soldered into a circuit. The end of the lead is wrapped around the contact area, and the alligator clip or heat sink is attached near the body of the device. When the soldering process begins, heat will travel up the lead toward the body, but the large surface area of the alligator clip will channel most of it

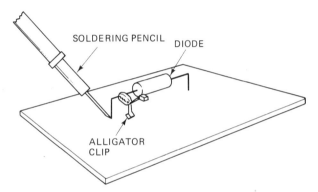

FIGURE 3-2 Attaching an alligator clip to the lead of a diode to effect thermal protection.

away from the internal semiconductor structure. Again, the heat sink must be large in surface area in comparison with the lead being soldered. Alligator clips are excellent for this purpose, because they do not need to be held in place. Alternately, you can grip the component lead near the body with long-nosed pliers, which will serve the same purpose. Of course, the use of pliers will dictate a hands-on heat-sinking operation. This can become awkward in some situations because one hand must grip the soldering iron while the other is normally used to apply the solder to the joint.

Local hobby stores often sell packages of clip-on heat sinks. They are normally grooved to fit around various sizes of conductors and are spring-loaded so they may be clipped in place. I have used them on a few occasions and find them to be more than adequate, but they are really the equivalent of a fancy alligator clip.

CONSTRUCTION TECHNIQUES

While most solid-state electronic circuits today are built on printed circuit board, this technique does not readily lend itself to the home workbench. It is possible to etch printed circuit boards from kits that are available from electronics outlets, but this can be a laborious process. Printed circuit board material must be purchased, along with a highly corrosive etching solution. Then the intended circuit wiring must be laid down on the copper material. This is done by drawing the conductors needed directly on the copper with an *antietch* pen. Wherever the antietch solution is applied, the copper will not be eaten away by the etching solution.

A more practical method for the electronics builder involves the use of perforated circuit board. This also is available in most electronics hobby outlets and is inexpensive when compared with printed circuit board material. The perforated board is made of a high-quality insulator, is relatively flexible, and contains evenly spaced perforations for the insertion of component leads. A typical board is shown in Fig. 3-3.

Obviously, there are no "built-in" conductor strips using perf board. All component interconnections are accomplished using point-to-point wiring techniques on the underside. Perf board is usually available in several different forms. All are made from the same material, but the difference lies in the spacing of the perforations. Wide-spaced perf board is best chosen for projects which use larger components, while the closer-spaced boards can be used for microminiature work.

Building electronic circuits on perf board is quite simple. Once you have arrived at a rough outline for component placement, the

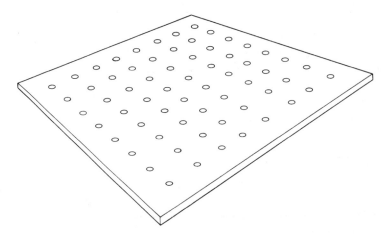

FIGURE 3-3 Unwired section of perforated circuit board.

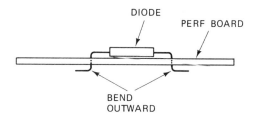

DIODE

PERF BOARD

BEND
OUTWARD

FIGURE 3-4   Mounting a diode on perf board.

leads of the various devices are inserted through the holes. They are then bent outward to temporarily secure them in place. This is shown in Fig. 3-4. After several components have been properly positioned, their leads may be wrapped together and soldered. You will want to place the components that are to be interconnected as close together as possible to avoid having to use separate sections of hookup wiring. For this reason, the physical layout of the circuit is highly important. When two component leads are wrapped together, only one solder joint is required. When two leads must be connected by a separate conductor, two joints are required. From an efficiency and dependability standpoint, you will want to design your circuit so that a minimum of solder connections is required.

How you actually mount the components will be determined in part by the desired physical size of the finished circuit. Some builders prefer to mount components mostly in the horizontal plane, while others will go with a vertical mounting technique. The latter method tends to produce a more compact finished circuit, since an equal amount of space may be used in both the horizontal and vertical planes. Figure 3-5 shows examples of both methods as applied to a single circuit. It can be seen that the horizontal method requires the board to be of larger size. However, it has a lower profile than when using the vertical method. When several circuit boards are required for a complex project and are to be interconnected, the space available in the mounting enclosure can most likely be better utilized by mounting the components vertically.

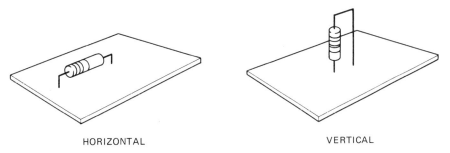

HORIZONTAL

VERTICAL

FIGURE 3-5   Examples of horizontal and vertical component mounting on perf board.

TOOLS AND TEST EQUIPMENT

Electronic circuit construction does not usually require a wide assortment of tools and test equipment. For the projects in this book, the builder will need a good soldering pencil, preferably one that is temperature regulated. A supply of resin core solder should be kept on hand at all times, along with a quantity of desoldering braid. This is a thin, narrow strip of many tiny copper conductors that have been woven together. When placed on a previously soldered joint and heated with a soldering pencil, the braid will suck solder away from the bond and allow the metal elements to be separated. Specialized desoldering tools are available which depend on air suction to remove the heated solder, but the desoldering braid is far less expensive and is often easier to work with.

The builder should have a minimum tool complement which consists of a pair of small diagonal cutters, needlenose pliers, and a small bench vise. This will complete the complement for the actual circuit board wiring. Additional tools will be needed for installation of the circuit boards in plastic and metal compartments. These can include small- and medium-sized Phillips and flathead screwdrivers, tin snips, a hand or electric drill, and a general assortment of nuts, bolts, and washers. A kit of *jeweler's screwdrivers* is always a welcome addition to any construction bench. They may be purchased at a local hardware store or from an electronics hobby outlet. While not mandatory, a set of nutdrivers will help with chassis assembly.

It is difficult to name all the extras which might be required from time to time to properly assemble some projects. Often, special tools and accessories will be purchased to suit the job. If you're in the process of stocking a workbench, I would suggest purchasing a quantity of epoxy cement, electrical tape, a small wirestripper, and a good tweezer. No workbench is complete without a good pocket knife which can be used to strip wire and remove unwanted solder globs and for a myriad of other purposes.

In addition to the nuts, bolts, and washers mentioned earlier, other hardware should include an assortment of rubber grommets, electronic terminal strips, metal spacers, self-tapping screws, and assorted lengths of stranded hookup wire. Again, all these items can be purchased locally and inexpensively.

From a test instrument standpoint, the most useful and universal item is the multimeter. This may also be called a volt-ohmmeter or simply an ohmmeter. Multimeter is a more accurate designation, however, as most of these instruments will read resistance in ohms, ac and dc voltage, and current. Figure 3-6 shows my multimeter, which is a precision instrument and is rather costly as these devices go. Multimeter cost is directly related to the accuracy of the instru-

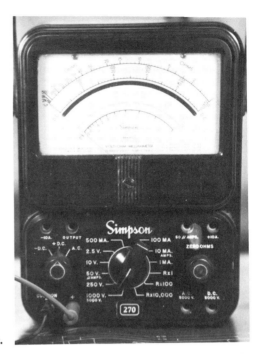

FIGURE 3-6 Good bench multimeter.

ment. Inexpensive multimeters present higher deviation levels which must be taken into account when performing some measurements. In electronic building applications, the multimeter will most often be used as a continuity tester. This involves turning the selector switch to the ohms position. A near-zero reading indicates continuity, while a reading of infinity denotes an open circuit or a break. When used as an ohmmeter, this device can indicate the values of resistors, checking them against their printed designations.

When used as a voltmeter, the builder may check supply and output voltages throughout the circuit, whether they be ac or dc. Current drains can also be monitored by placing the multimeter in series with a power supply. In all three modes of operation, several different scales are provided for monitoring different value ranges.

Other test instruments may be incorporated in your bench complement to perform more exhaustive checks on electronic circuits. They can include an oscilloscope, audio-frequency generator, radio-frequency generator, transistor-diode checker, etc. Since the main topic of this book is diodes, it is appropriate to point out that most of these components can be checked for good-bad operation by the universal instrument, the multimeter. By placing the negative probe on the anode connection of a diode and the positive probe on the cathode lead, a test is conducted which should yield a very low resistance (X_1 scale) when set up to read ohms. Now reverse the leads, and a very high resistance should be obtained. If this two-part test results in the readings described here, then the diode is probably good. If a high or low resistance is read in both positions, then there is a good possibility the component is defective. Transistors can be checked in a similar manner, as can other components.

The purpose of this text is not to describe in detail the operation of a multimeter or other test instruments. But you will find that the multimeter will be called to service again and again and is an absolute must for every building project.

THE COST FACTOR

It is not necessary to purchase the highest-quality tools and test instruments offered on the market today. By the same token, it is not recommended that you purchase the cheapest ones either. As a general rule of thumb, tools must be of the proper size and adequate quality to get the job done. Extremely inexpensive diagonal cutters may seem like a real bargain, but these types are typically very stiff and difficult to operate in the close confines of a small electronic circuit board. Whereas the inexpensive cutters may cost less than $3, top-of-the-line versions may be priced at $10 or more. However, you will be using this tool quite often, so a higher grade is certainly warranted. Since this is one of the more basic and mandatory tools for an electronics workbench, you will certainly want to consider purchasing a higher-quality version. Your money will be well spent.

As far as screwdrivers are concerned, I have found that the $1 specials which are seen advertised daily work reasonably well for most electronic assembly. If you intend to use these tools for other than electronic applications, again, higher-quality types would probably be the better investment. The same criteria outlined for diagonal cutters apply equally to the purchase of needlenose pliers. This tool will be used to stabilize components and remove small pieces of metal from electronic circuits and for many other purposes. Therefore, a high-quality tool is recommended because of the more uniform gripping surface and better operational characteristics.

There is still quite a bit of controversy over which type of drill is best for electronics work: hand or electric. The actual selection will depend on the experience of the builder. A hand drill provides a higher degree of precision in that speed can be linearly varied. If an electric drill is preferred, make certain it is a variable-speed type. One begins drilling a hole at a slow speed and then steps up the pace once the initial cavity has been formed. Hand drills are becoming increasingly more difficult to find, especially in rural areas, while electric drills are available almost everywhere. Possibly the best arrangement would be to have both on hand. The electric drill could then be used for metal work and heavier applications, and the hand drill would be brought into play when it is necessary to perform work on the delicate circuit board itself.

Overall, the selection of tools and test instruments is often a trial and error process. Tools must fit the experience and style of the builder, so needs will vary. Should you purchase a tool that is not quite suited to your needs, try to define its faults and then purchase another which corrects them. To avoid unnecessary expense, it is an excellent idea to at least hold and operate (on a dry run basis) your intended purchase. Any stiffness in moving parts or unusual handling difficulties can often be detected by this simple process.

Caution: Be very wary of inexpensive tools and instruments which are to be used for high-voltage applications. An inexpensive screwdriver may be fitted with a handle that is not properly insulated to protect from these potentials. Stay away from models with wooden handles. They are very dangerous when used around moderate to high voltage, especially in damp environments. Should moisture infiltrate the handle, very little insulation protection will be provided. This same note of caution applies to the handles or grips of all other tools which could come in contact with moderate to high voltage potentials.

Some inexpensive multimeters are capable of measuring ac and dc potentials of up to 5000 V or more. This would lead one to believe that they have been designed for high-voltage measurement purposes. This is often untrue. The problem here lies in the insulation of the test probes. While the meter may measure potentials of several kilovolts or more, the probe handles and conductor insulation may be rated at 600 V or less. This means that the technician could be placed in a very dangerous situation when gripping the probe handles while they are across high voltage potentials. While most of the projects in this book do not or cannot be operated in the multikilovolt level, some can, and others may be modified to do so. Since there is always a possibility that any multimeter you purchase may be eventually used to read these high potentials, it is necessary to inquire about the rated insulation level of the device and its probes. In most instances, an inexpensive meter can be safely used for measuring high voltage by simply replacing the original probe leads with those of a higher quality that are rated to withstand the maximum measurement potential of the instrument.

THE ART OF CIRCUIT BUILDING

Now that the basics have been discussed, it is important to talk about the actual building of a circuit. Here, certain work habits are required for the best chance of success. I have been building my own circuits for over 20 years, and even now there is always a feeling of anticipation when power is first applied to a completed project. Will it work? It is often the case that a fairly complex circuit, one which tests your construction skills, will work the first time, while some of the simpler ones won't. Why is this? Generally, the builder will take more time in checking every connection during the building of the complex circuit because there is more room for error. When building simpler circuits, it is sometimes easy to become a bit casual about its completion, and mistakes can occur. Put another way, you anticipate a wiring error in a highly complex circuit and don't in a simple one. For this reason, it is important to build all circuits in the same manner, checking solder connections, component polarities, etc. If you do this every time, your chances for immediate success when power is applied will be excellent.

It has already been stated that the major cause of home-built circuit problems is poor solder connections. The second major cause would have to be the failure on the part of the builder to take the time required to finish a project. All too often there is a mad rush to slap the components on the circuit board, make hasty solder joints, and then apply power. Circuit building is a matter of patience. As you practice this art, your assembly time will certainly decrease, but you should never be rushed. Never set a goal for yourself to finish a project, say, within 3 or 4 h. This puts you in a position of racing the clock, and there's a much higher chance of errors occurring. A project which requires 3 h for one builder to complete may take you twice as long or half as long. As your building experience accumulates, you will most likely be able to view a schematic drawing and have a rough idea of how long it will take to complete the circuit. But this is not always the case, especially with persons who are new to this pursuit.

Another major cause of circuit failure is fatigue. It is very difficult for most persons to sit at a workbench for hours on end, accurately placing, connecting, and soldering tiny components. Even in the most comfortable working conditions, there can be a fair amount of eye strain, and heavy requirements are placed upon mental concentration. I find that I am most efficient when I take a 10- or 15-min break every 30 or 45 min. You may be able to go longer, or you may require breaks more often. This is a factor that varies from person to person. When building electronic circuits, it is easy for what I call intensity to set in. The builder becomes wrapped up in the circuitry to such an extent that nothing else seems to exist, and there is a conscious or subconscious push to finish. It's at times like these that a break is required. Get completely away from the workbench and don't even think electronics for 10 min or so. A breath of fresh air and perhaps a cup of coffee will help you to return to a relaxed state. This is the best frame of mind for successful circuit building.

Naturally, it is mandatory to arrange for a comfortable working area, one that is free of components and materials that are not to be used for the particular project under construction. A good overhead light is needed, along with the tools and other equipment which will be required. Make certain that you have *all* materials on hand to finish a particular project *before* you begin. Projects which are started with less than a full complement of components and/or assembly tools may never be completed. It seems relatively simple to build a project by omitting those circuit portions for which parts have not yet been obtained. This is always done with the intention of wiring in the missing components at a later date. When complex circuits are involved, however, it may be very difficult to skip a whole circuit portion and still allow adequate mounting space, connections, etc., for the missing elements. Most electronic circuits will be mounted in a protective enclosure after they are completed and tested for proper operation. However, a half-finished circuit that must sit on a workbench for weeks while awaiting the arrival of a component or two is highly subject to accidental damage. Building an electronic circuit is like writing a term paper. All research must be done before the effort is undertaken.

SAFETY

Safety procedures must be observed at all times when involved in electronics circuit building. While some circuits operate at relatively low voltage potentials, others may involve dangerous or even lethal values. Then, too, even a small soldering pencil can cause severe burns. A well-stocked first aid kit is mandatory for any electronics workbench, along with a knowledge of first aid procedures. Minor cuts and scrapes are nothing to be ignored either. Remember, there will most likely be a fair amount of metal shavings and razor-sharp component lead sections which have been clipped away during the soldering procedure. Should any of these enter even a small break in the skin, a severe cutting action may be set up which will deepen the wound and quite possibly cause infection. To avoid some of these hazards, I often wear tight-fitting rubber gloves when working on some circuits. Your first aid kit should contain the usual assortment of antiseptics, Band-Aids, tweezers, etc., and should be immediately available.

Diode rectifiers are commonly used in dc power supplies, all of which can present lethal potentials. This even applies to low-voltage power supplies whose output potentials are less than 25 V. Remember, nearly all these will receive power directly from the ac line. Household ac current is a major source of severe electrical shock and kills many people each year. Anyone who must test, troubleshoot, or align a dc power supply with a high output potential must take every precaution to avoid contact with the active circuit. There is no such thing as a slight electrical shock when dealing with potentials of 500 V or more. For this reason, it is an excellent idea to always have an assistant present to aid you in case an accident should occur. One has only to witness the damage that can be done to the human body by moderate- to high-voltage sources to realize the importance of electrical safety.

The practice of safety brings us back to a point that was touched upon earlier: not working past your point of mental concentration. When the builder becomes mentally and/or physically fatigued, reactions are slowed, and mistakes are made. If the mistake involves placing a portion of the human body in contact with a potentially lethal source, then building has ceased to be a relaxing exercise and is instead a life-threatening gamble.

Every home electronics shop should be equipped with a master circuit breaker. When this is tripped, *all* power to the work area is disrupted. Every member of your household should know how to operate this switch to remove any voltage potential in the event of an accident. One hears repeatedly of electrical accidents occurring in which persons attempting to give aid to the injured party have been seriously injured or killed themselves owing to the fact that the power was still on.

The purpose of the latter discussion is not to discourage electronics experimentation. When proper safety rules are followed, this is a very safe pursuit. But when high voltage is involved, there is little room for mistakes. Generally, it is not the beginner to electronics experimentation who suffers an electrical shock of severe proportions. Rather it is the experienced technician who most often falls prey. It can be theorized that familiarity and even complacency is the culprit in the latter group. After years of working on electronic circuits, the once-practiced safety precautions are often laid by the wayside, and an accident occurs. It is not enough to respect high voltage potentials; it is mandatory that you maintain a deathly fear of its consequences.

SUMMARY

The assembly of electronic circuits in the home workshop is a pleasant and rewarding pursuit, but it can also be a very frustrating experience when proper building techniques are not practiced. The procedures outlined in this chapter may seem complicated at first, especially to those who have not had a great deal of electronics building experience, but the process is both simple and straightforward and is generally learned quickly.

No pursuit can be carried out efficiently without the proper tools. Fortunately, most electronic building projects, varied in scope though they may be, do not require a tremendously large assortment. All can be purchased locally, along with most types of test equipment.

Safety is a prime requisite for the continuation of electronic circuit building. It must be practiced constantly, as even an instantaneous variance can result in injury. Most safety rules governing electronic circuit construction are common-sense-oriented and will become a natural part of the building process after a short period of time.

The culmination of all the procedures outlined in this chapter will be a successful construction routine which will allow the builder to produce finished circuits that will operate in proper accordance with their design. Additionally, these circuits will continue to function in a reliable manner throughout their useful life.

4

Rectification and
Power Supplies

Rectification is described as the changing of an alternating current (ac) to a unidirectional or direct current (dc). The normal *PN* junction diode is well suited for this purpose, as it conducts very heavily when forward biased (low-resistance direction) and only slightly when reverse biased (high-resistance direction).

Figure 4-1 is a block diagram of a power supply showing an ac input to and a dc output from a block labeled positive power supply and filter network. Although this figure shows a power supply that provides a unidirectional current which causes a positive voltage output, it might well be designed to furnish a negative voltage output.

The question of why a change of ac to dc is necessary probably arises. Put simply, the answer is that for proper operation, many electronic circuits depend on dc. As already pointed out, the *PN* junction diode conducts more easily in one direction than in the other. Transistors and electron tubes are also unidirectional, and a constantly alternating source voltage would be undesirable.

Before describing how an ac input is converted into a dc output, the definition of *load* as it applies to power supplies must be understood. Load is the current supplied to the power-consuming device or devices connected to the power supply. The power-consuming device needs voltage and current for proper operation, and this voltage and current is supplied by the power supply. The power-consuming device

FIGURE 4-1 Positive voltage output from an ac input.

may be a simple resistor or one or more electronic circuits using resistors, capacitors, coils, and active devices.

HALF-WAVE RECTIFIER

Figure 4-2 shows the *PN* junction diode functioning as a half-wave rectifier. A half-wave rectifier is one that uses only half of the input cycle to produce an output.

The induced voltage across L_2 (the transformer secondary) will be as shown in Fig. 4-1. The dots on the transformer indicate points of the same polarity. During that portion of the input cycle which is going positive (solid line), CR_1, the *PN* junction diode, will be forward biased, and current will flow through the circuit. L_2, acting as the source voltage, will have current flowing from the top to the bottom. This current then flows up through R_L, causing a voltage drop across R_L equal to the value of current flowing times the value of R_L. This voltage drop will be positive at the top of R_L with respect to its other side, and the output will therefore be a positive voltage with respect to ground. It is common practice for the end of a resistor receiving current to be given a sign representing a negative polarity of voltage, and the end of the resistor through which current leaves is assigned a positive polarity of voltage. The voltage drop across R_L, plus the voltage drops across the conducting diode and L_2, will equal the applied

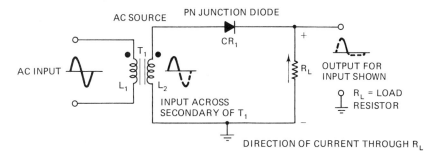

FIGURE 4-2 Positive voltage output half-wave *PN* junction diode rectifier.

voltage. Although the output voltage will nearly equal the peak input voltage, it cannot reach this value due to the voltage drops, no matter how small, across CR_1 and L_2.

The negative half cycle of the input is illustrated by the broken line. When the negative half cycle is felt on CR_1, the PN junction diode is reverse biased. The reverse current will be very small, but it will exist. The voltage resulting from the reverse current, as shown below the line in the output, is exaggerated in Fig. 4-2 to bring out the point of its existence. Although only one cycle of input is shown in this figure, it should be realized that the action described above continually repeats itself as long as there is an input.

By reversing the diode connection in Fig. 4-2 (having the anode on the right instead of the left), the output would now become a negative voltage. The current would be going from the top of R_L toward the bottom, making the output at the top of R_L negative in respect to the bottom or ground.

The same negative output can be obtained from this figure if the reference point (ground) is changed from the bottom (where it is shown) to the top or cathode-connected end of the resistor. The bottom of R_L is shown as being negative in respect to the top, and reading the output voltage from the "hot" side of the resistor to ground would result in a negative voltage output.

The half-wave rectifier will normally indicate improper functioning in one of two manners: There is no output, or the output is low. The *no-output* condition can be caused by no input: The fuse has blown, the transformer primary or secondary winding is open, the PN junction diode is open, or the load is open.

The low-output condition might be caused by an aged diode. A check of both forward and reverse resistance of the diode may reveal the condition of the diode. Low output can be the result of an increased forward resistance or a decreased reverse resistance of the diode.

It is necessary to check the ac input voltage to see if it is of the correct value. A low input voltage will result in a low output voltage. A check of the transformer secondary voltage should be made to see if it is of the correct value also, as a low secondary voltage will also result in a low output voltage.

By removing the input voltage, the troubleshooter can make resistance checks of the components. Is the primary open? The secondary open? Has the diode increased in forward resistance value or decreased in reverse resistance value? Is the diode open? Has the load resistance become shorted? Do the components show signs of excessive heat dissipation? Have they become discolored? Does energizing the circuit and putting an ammeter in series with the load make the load current excessive?

All these questions should be answered when troubleshooting

the half-wave rectifier. If a problem is discovered in the rectifier, one should then determine if the cause is a local one (in the rectifier itself) or due to some changes in the following circuitry, such as the power supply filter components or changing load impedance. While it is important that the problem be repaired, elimination of the cause of the problem is of greater importance.

FULL-WAVE RECTIFIER

The *PN* junction diode works just as well in a full-wave rectifier circuit, as shown in Fig. 4-3. The circuit shown has a negative voltage output. However, it might just as well have a positive voltage output. This can be accomplished by either changing the reference point (ground side of R_L) or by reversing the diodes in the circuit.

The ac input is felt across the secondary winding of T_1. This winding is center tapped as shown; the center of the secondary is at ground potential. This seems to be a good time to define ground as a reference point which is of no particular polarity. When the polarity is such that the top of T_1 secondary is negative, the bottom is positive. At this time, the center tap, as shown, has two polarities, positive with respect to the top half of the winding and negative with respect to the bottom half of the winding. When the secondary winding is positive at the top, the bottom is negative, and the center tap is negative with respect to the top and positive with respect to the bottom. What is the polarity of the reference point (ground)? The answer must be in terms of "with respect to." For each alternation of the input, one of the diodes will be forward biased and the other one reverse biased.

For ease of explanation, the negative alternation will be considered when the rectifier current is initially energized by the ac source. CR_1 will be forward biased (negative voltage felt on its cathode), and CR_2 will be reverse biased (a positive voltage felt on its cathode). Therefore, the top of T_1 secondary must be negative with respect to the bottom. When forward bias is applied to CR_1, it conducts heavily from cathode to anode (dashed arrow), down through R_L (this current flow creates a voltage drop across R_L), negative at the top with respect to the bottom or ground side of R_L. The current passing through R_L is

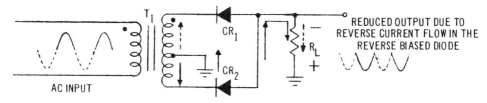

FIGURE 4-3 Unfiltered negative output full-wave rectifier.

returned to CR_1 by going through the grounded center tap and up the upper section of the center-tapped secondary winding of T_1. This completes the first alternation of the input cycle. The second alternation of the input now is of such polarity as to forward-bias CR_2 (a negative voltage at the bottom of T_1 secondary winding with respect to ground). CR_1 is now reverse biased; CR_2 conducts, and current moves in the same direction through R_L (solid arrow), top to bottom, back through the lower half of the center-tapped secondary to CR_2. One may wonder why current does not flow from the anode of one of the diodes through the anode to cathode of the other diode. The answer is simple; it does. However, current flow through a reverse-biased diode is very slight due to the high resistance of the diode when reverse biased. This rectifier has a slightly reduced output because of the reverse current flow.

As can be seen in the output waveform of Fig. 4-3, there are two pulses of dc out for every cycle of ac in; this is a full-wave recification. Current flow through R_L is in the same direction no matter which diode is conducting. The positive-going alternation of the input allows one diode to be forward biased, and the negative-going alternation of the input allows the other diode to be forward biased. The output for the full-wave rectifier shown is a negative voltage measured from the top of R_L to ground.

As in the half-wave rectifier, there can be two indications of a problem: *no output* or *low output*. No-output conditions are indications of no input, shorted load circuits, open primary winding, an open or shorted secondary winding, or defective diodes. Low-output conditions are possible indications of aging diodes, open diodes, or opens in either half of the secondary winding (allowing the circuit to act as a half-wave rectifier).

The method for troubleshooting the full-wave rectifier is the same as that used for the half-wave rectifier. Check voltages of both primary and secondary windings, check current flow, and when the circuit is de-energized, take resistance measurements. Shorted turns in the secondary windings give a lower-voltage output, and possibly shorted turns in the primary winding will produce a lower-voltage input. (Shorted turns are hard to detect with an ohmmeter; they are more easily detected by taking a voltage reading across various terminals of the energized transformer.)

BRIDGE RECTIFIER

Now the PN junction diode will be described as it is used in a bridge rectifier circuit. Figure 4-4 shows such a circuit capable of producing a positive output voltage. When the ac input is applied across the secondary winding of T_1, it will forward-bias diodes CR_1 and CR_3 or

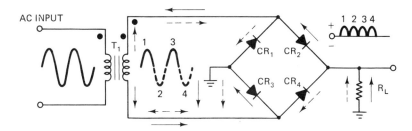

FIGURE 4-4 *PN* junction diode in a bridge rectifier circuit.

CR_2 and CR_4. When the top of the transformer is positive with respect to the bottom, as illustrated in Fig. 4-4 by the designation number 1, both CR_1 and CR_2 will feel this positive voltage. CR_1 will have a positive voltage on its cathode, a reverse bias condition, and CR_2 will have a positive voltage on its anode, a forward bias condition. At this same time, the bottom of the secondary winding will be negative with respect to the top, placing a negative voltage on the anode of CR_3 (a reverse bias condition) and on the cathode of CR_4 (a forward bias condition).

During the half cycle of the input designated by the number 1 in Fig. 4-4, it is found that CR_2 and CR_4 are forward biased and will therefore conduct heavily. The conducting path is shown by the solid arrows, from the source (the secondary winding of T_1) through CR_4 to ground, up through R_L, making the top of R_L positive with respect to the ground end, to the junction of CR_2 and CR_3. CR_2, being forward biased, offers the path of least resistance to current flow, and this is the path current will take to get back to the source.

During the alternation designated by the number 2 in Fig. 4-4, indicated by the dashed arrows, the top of the secondary winding is going negative, while the bottom is going positive. The negative voltage at the top is felt by both CR_1 and CR_2, forward-biasing CR_1 and reverse-biasing CR_2. The positive voltage on the bottom of T_1 secondary is felt by CR_3 and CR_4, forward-biasing CR_3 and reverse-biasing CR_4. Current flow, starting at the source (T_1 secondary winding), is through CR_1 to ground, up through R_L (the same direction as when CR_2 and CR_4 were conducting), making the top of R_L positive with respect to its grounded end, to the junction of CR_2 and CR_3. This time, CR_3 is forward biased, and current takes this path to return to its source.

As can be seen, the diodes in the bridge circuit operate in pairs; first one pair (CR_1 and CR_3) conducts heavily, and then the other pair (CR_2 and CR_4) conducts heavily. As shown in the output waveform, we get one pulse out for every half cycle of the input, or two pulses out for every cycle in. This is the same as for the full-wave rectifier circuit explained previously.

Bridge Rectifier **49**

The bridge circuit will also indicate a malfunction in one of two manners: It has no output or a low output. The causes for both conditions are the same as they were for the half- or full-wave rectifier. If any one of the diodes opens, the circuit will act as a half-wave rectifier, with a resultant lower output voltage.

POWER SUPPLY FILTERS

As previously indicated, the operation of most electronic circuits is dependent on a direct-current source. It has been illustrated how alternating current can be changed into a pulsating direct current, that is, a current that is always positive or negative with respect to ground, although it is not of a steady value. Instead, it has *ripple.*

Ripple can be defined as the departure of the waveform of a rectifier from pure dc. It is the amplitude excursions, positive and negative, of a waveform from the pure dc value (the alternating component of the rectifier voltage). Ripple contains two factors which must be considered: frequency and amplitude. Ripple frequency, in the rectifiers that have been presented, is either the same as line frequency for the half-wave rectifier or twice the line frequency for the full-wave rectifier.

In the half-wave rectifier, one pulse of dc output was generated for one cycle of ac input. The ripple frequency is the same as the input frequency. In the full-wave rectifiers (center tapped and bridge), two pulses of dc output were produced for each cycle of ac input. The ripple frequency here is twice that of the line frequency. With a 60-Hz input frequency, there will be a 60-Hz ripple frequency in the output of the half-wave rectifier and a 120-Hz ripple frequency in the output of the full-wave rectifier.

The amplitude of the ripples in the output of a rectifier circuit will give us a measure of the effectiveness of the filter being used, or the ripple factor. The ripple factor is defined as the ratio of the rms value of the ac component to the average dc value, or

$$r = \frac{E_{rms}}{E_{dc}}$$

The lower the ripple factor, the more effective the filter. The term *percent of ripple* may be used. This is different from the ripple factor only because the figure arrived at in the ripple factor formula is multiplied by 100 to give us the percent figure, or

$$\frac{E_{rms}}{E_{dc}} \times 100$$

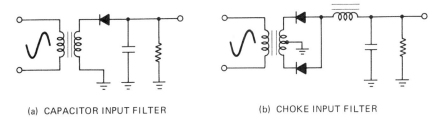

(a) CAPACITOR INPUT FILTER   (b) CHOKE INPUT FILTER

FIGURE 4-5   Filter circuit.

In both formulas given, E_{rms} is the rms value of ripple voltage, and E_{dc} is the dc value (average value) of the output voltage.

Filter circuits used in power supplies are usually low-pass filters. (A low-pass filter is a network which passes all frequencies below a specified frequency with little or no loss but is highly discriminate against all higher frequencies.) The filtering is done through the use of resistors or inductors and capacitors. The purpose of power supply filters is to smooth out the ripple contained in the pulses of dc obtained from the rectifier circuit while increasing the average output voltage or current.

Filter circuits used in power supplies are of two general types: capacitor input and choke input. There are several combinations that may be used, although they are referred to by different names (pi, RC, L section, etc.). The element closest electrically to the rectifier determines the basic type of filter being used.

Figure 4-5 depicts the basic types. In (a), a capacitor shunts the load resistor, therein bypassing the majority of ripple current which passes through the series elements. In (b), an inductor (choke) in series with the load resistor opposes any change in current in the circuit. The capacitor input filter will keep the output voltage at a higher level compared to a choke input. The choke input will provide a steadier current under changing load conditions. From this it can be seen that a capacitor input filter would be used where voltage is the prime factor, and the choke input filter is used where a steady flow of current is required.

CAPACITOR INPUT FILTER

First, an analysis will be made of the simple capacitor input filter depicted in Fig. 4-6(a). The output of the rectifier, without filtering, is shown in (b), and the output after filtering is illustrated in (c). Without the capacitor, the output across R_L will be pulses, as previously

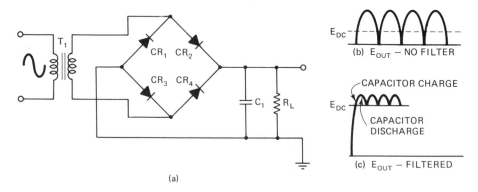

(a)

(b) E_{OUT} – NO FILTER

(c) E_{OUT} – FILTERED

FIGURE 4-6 Low-voltage power supply with simple capacitor filter.

described. The average value of these pulses would be the E_{dc} output of the rectifier.

With the addition of the capacitor, the majority of the pulse changes are bypassed through the capacitor and around R_L. As the first pulse appears across the capacitor, changing it from negative to positive, bottom to top, the peak voltage is developed across the capacitor. When the first half cycle has reached its peak and starts its negative-going excursion, the capacitor will start to discharge through R_L, maintaining the current through R_L in its original direction and thereby holding the voltage across R_L at a higher value than its unfiltered load. Before the capacitor can fully discharge, the positive excursion of the next half cycle is nearing its peak, recharging the capacitor. As the pulse again starts to go negative, the capacitor starts to discharge once again. The positive-going excursion of the next half cycle comes in and recharges the capacitor. This action continues as long as the circuit is in operation.

The charge path for the capacitor is through the transformer secondary and the conducting diodes, and the discharge path is through the load resistor. The reactance of the capacitor at the line frequency is small compared to R_L, which allows the changes to bypass R_L, and effectively only pure dc appears across R_L.

This illustrates the use of an RC time constant. If the value of C_1 or R_L were such that the discharge time was the same or less than that of the charge time, we would have no filtering action. The larger the values of C_1 and R_L, the longer the time constant and the lower the ripple factor. The charge time of the capacitor is the RC values of the capacitor, the conducting diodes, and the transformer secondary. The impedance offered by these elements is very small when compared to the impedance in the discharge path of the capacitor (the value of R_L). The output voltage is practically the peak value of the input voltage. This circuit provides very good filtering action for low currents but results in little filtering in higher-current power supplies due to the smaller resistance of the load.

CHOKE INPUT FILTER

The next filter to be analyzed is the choke input filter or the L-section filter. Figure 4-7 shows this filter and the resultant output of the rectifier after filtering has taken place. The series inductor, L (choke), will oppose rapid changes in current. The output voltage of this filter is less than that of the capacitor input filter, since the choke is in series with the output impedance. The parallel combination of R_L and C in connection with L smooths out the peaks of the pulses and results in a steady, although reduced, output.

The inductance chokes off the peaks of the alternating components of the rectified waveform, and the dc voltage is the average or dc value of the rectified wave. The choke input filter allows a continuous flow of current from the rectifier diodes rather than the pulsating current flow, as seen in the capacitor input filter. The X_L of the choke reduces the ripple voltage by opposing any change in current during either the rapid increases in current during the positive excursions of the pulse or decreases in current during the negative excursions. This keeps a steady current flowing to the load throughout the entire cycle. The pulsating voltage developed across the capacitor is maintained at a relatively constant value approaching the average value of input voltage because of this steady current flow.

The filtering action of the choke input filter can be enhanced by using more than one such section. Figure 4-8 shows two sections with representative waveforms approximating the shape of the voltage with respect to ground at different points in the filter networks.

While this figure shows two choke input sections being used as a multiple-section filter, more sections may be added as desired. While multiple-section filters do reduce the ripple content (and they are found

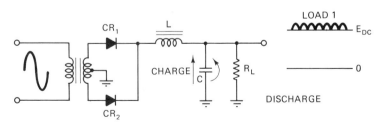

FIGURE 4-7 *L*-section (choke input) filter showing current waveforms.

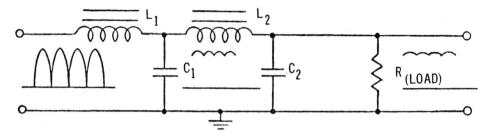

FIGURE 4-8   Multiple-section choke input filter with representative waveforms.

in applications where only a minimum ripple content can be tolerated in the output voltage), they also result in reduced regulation. The additional sections add more resistance in series with the power supply, which results in increased voltage variations in the output when the load current varies.

PI FILTER

The pi filter (called this because of its resemblance to the Greek letter pi) is a combination of the simple capacitor input filter and the choke filter. It is shown in Fig. 4-9.

The resistor, R, is known as a bleeder resistor and is found in practically all power supplies. The purpose of this resistor is twofold. When the equipment has been working and is then turned off, it provides a discharge path for the capacitor, preventing a possible shock hazard. It also provides a fixed load no matter what equipment is connected to the power supply. It is also possible to use this resistor as a voltage-dividing network through the use of appropriate taps.

The pi filter is basically a capacitor input filter with the addition of an L-section filter. The majority of the filtering action takes place across C_1, which charges through the conducting diode(s) and discharges through R, L, and C_2. As in the simple capacitor input filter, the charge time is very fast compared to the discharge time. The inductor smooths out the peaks of the current pulses felt across C_2, thereby providing additional filtering action. The voltage across C_2,

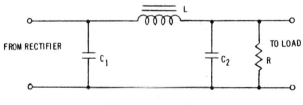

FIGURE 4-9   Pi filter.

54   Rectification and Power Supplies

since C_2 is in parallel with the output, is the output voltage of the power supply. Although the voltage output is lower in this filter than it would be if taken across C_1 and the load, the amount of ripple is greatly reduced.

Even though C_1 will charge to the peak voltage of the input when the diodes are conducting and discharge through R when they are cut off, the inductor is also in the discharge path and opposes any changes in load current. The voltage-dividing action of L and C_2 is responsible for the lower output voltage in the pi filter when compared to the voltage available across C_1.

In Fig. 4-9, the charge path for both C_1 and C_2 is through the transformer secondary, through the capacitors, and in the case of C_2 through L. Both charge paths are through the conducting diode. However, the discharge path for C_1 is through R and L, while the discharge path for C_2 is through R only. How fast the input capacitor, C_1, discharges is primarily determined by the ohmic value of R. The discharge time of the capacitors is directly proportional to the value of R. If C_1 has very little chance to discharge, the output voltage will be high. For lower values of R_1, the discharge rate is faster, and the output voltage will decrease. With a lower value of resistance, the current will be greater, and the capacitor will discharge further. The E output is the average value of dc, and the faster the discharge time, the lower the average value of dc and the lower the E out.

RC CAPACITOR INPUT FILTER

While the pi filter just discussed had an inductor placed between two capacitors, the inductor can be replaced by a resistor, as shown in Fig. 4-10. The main difference in operation between this pi filter and the one previously discussed is the reaction of an inductor to ac when compared to the resistor. In the former filter, the combination of the reactances of L and C_2 to ac was such as to smooth dc output.

In Fig. 4-10, both the ac and dc components of rectified current pass through R_1. The output voltage is reduced due to the voltage drop

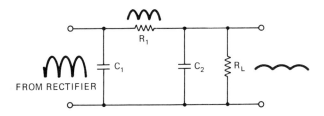

FIGURE 4-10 Capacitor input filter and associated waveforms.

across R_1, and the higher the current, the greater this voltage drop. This filter is effective in high-voltage/low-current applications. As in choke input filters, the capacitor input filters shown may be multiplied; i.e., identical sections may be added in series.

The choice of a filter for a particular use is a design problem, but the purpose and operation of filters should be understood because of their importance in the proper operation of equipment following the power supply.

COMBINATIONAL VOLTAGE SUPPLIES

Power supplies found in modern electronics equipment must supply a great variety of voltages and current. The need for combination power supplies becomes evident when equipment requirements are voltage in ranges of −5, −15, −55, +5, +120, +2400, and −580 V for a typical oscilloscope or −90 V at 6 mA, +28 V at 180 mA and 580 ms, +130 V at 315 mA, and 250 V at 37 mA, as used in the low-voltage power supply for a typical radio transceiver.

The necessity of having a power supply capable of delivering a high-voltage/low-current output, a low-voltage/high-current output, and a high-voltage/high-current output simultaneously is the reason for having combinational power supplies. Two basic combinations will be presented here: the full-wave bridge and the full-wave full-wave.

FULL-WAVE BRIDGE

Figure 4-11 is an example of the full-wave bridge combinational power supply. Figure 4-11(a) shows a simplified schematic drawing, and (b) shows the entire schematic, including the filtering network. It is a typical arrangement of the full-wave bridge combination supply, quite often called the economy power supply.

In Fig. 4-11(b), CR_1 and CR_3 form the full-wave rectifier circuit, and C_2A, C_2B, and L_2 form the filter network. R_1 is a current-limiting resistor used to protect the diodes from surge currents. R_4 is the bleeder resistor and also assures that the power supply has a minimum load at all times. CR_1 and CR_4 form the bridge rectifier circuit, with L_1, R_2, C_1A, and C_1B doing the filtering. R_3 is a bleeder resistor and assures that the bridge always has a minimum load. Each circuit in itself works in the conventional manner. Troubleshooting is the same as for other power supplies covered, entailing the *no-output/low-output* factors.

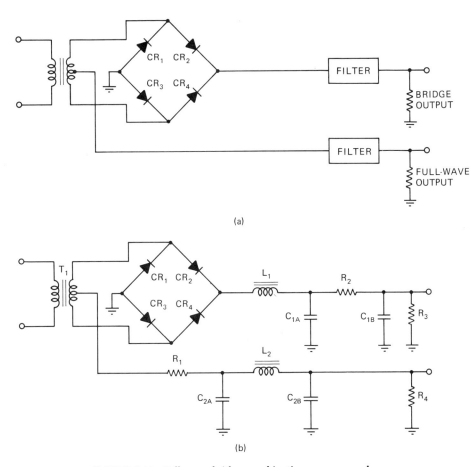

(a)

(b)

FIGURE 4-11　Full-wave bridge combination power supply.

FULL-WAVE FULL-WAVE

Figure 4-12 illustrates a full-wave full-wave combinational power supply with positive and negative outputs. It has one primary distinguishing feature as compared to a bridge circuit: the center-tapped transformer secondary. The components associated with the negative voltage output are CR_1, CR_3, L_2, C_2, and R_2, while CR_2, CR_4, L_1, C_1, and R_1 are the components in the positive voltage output. Transformer T_1 is a component common to both supplies.

The operation of each full-wave rectifier is identical. The operation will be explained once again as a refresher. When point A is negative with respect to ground, point B will be positive. This condition causes both CR_1 and CR_4 to conduct. Both these diodes are associated with a different full-wave rectifier. The negative power supply will

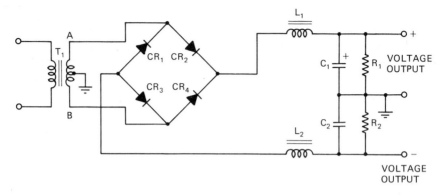

FIGURE 4-12 Full-wave full-wave combinational power supply with positive and negative output voltages.

be described first. This is the one associated with the conduction of CR_1. Current through CR_1 flows through L_2, C_2, and R_2 and completes the path via ground to the transformer center tap and thence to A. This is the path during the first half cycle while CR_1 is conducting. At the same time this action is taking place, CR_4 is conducting in the positive power supply. Since point B is positive and the lower half of the transformer secondary acts as a source, current from point B to ground flows up through C_1, charging it as shown, L_1, CR_4, and back to the source. When the polarities at points A and B are reversed, point A now being positive and point B being negative with respect to ground, the conducting diodes are now CR_3 in the negative supply and CR_2 in the positive supply.

Again, taking the negative supply first, CR_3 conducts, and the current path, from point B and back to point B, is through CR_3, L_2, up through C_2 in the same manner as when CR_1 was conducting, to ground, and through the center tap of the transformer to point B. This completes the full cycle of operation for the negative supply, and CR_1 and CR_3 will be conducting alternately as long as there is an input.

At the time CR_3 is conducting in the negative power supply, CR_2 is conducting in the positive power supply. Current from point A back to point A is going down the upper half of the transformer secondary to ground, up through C_1 and L_1, through CR_2, and back to point A. Again, the charge path for C_1 is the same as it was when CR_4 was conducting.

While it has been said that when troubleshooting the combinational power supply the problems to look for are of the no-output/low-output type, it should be realized that in the full-wave bridge combinational power supply, a low output can occur in either section, or the voltage out of the full-wave rectifier can be normal while the bridge rectifier might indicate a low output. If the load currents are not excessive and the filter components have checked out, the defective diodes, in the first case, would be assumed to be CR_1 or CR_3 and in the second case to be CR_2 or CR_4.

VOLTAGE MULTIPLIERS

Figure 4-13 depicts a simple half-wave rectifier circuit that is capable of delivering a voltage increase (more voltage output than voltage input), providing the current being drawn is low. It is shown that it is possible to get a larger voltage out of a simple half-wave rectifier as long as the current is low. If the current demand increases, the output voltage will decrease. This can best be explained by the use of the RC time constant. The charge time for the circuit in this figure is very fast, since the circuit elements in the capacitor's charge path are the diode, CR_1, the surge resistor R, and the secondary of the transformer. These elements combine to form a very low impedance, since CR_1 is conducting during the charge time and the value of R_1 is about 20 Ω. In comparison, the discharge path for the capacitor is through the load, which offers an impedance several hundred times higher than that of the charge path. The lower the load impedance, the greater the current. If the discharge path for the capacitor offers a lower impedance, the capacitor will discharge further, lowering the output voltage.

Rectifier circuits that can be used to double, triple, and quadruple the input voltage will be discussed. All these circuits have one thing in common. They use the charge stored on capacitors to increase the output voltage. Figure 4-14 is a block diagram of a voltage multiplier circuit. The input is ac, and the output is dc multiple.

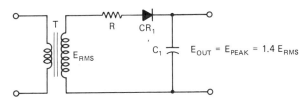

FIGURE 4-13 Simple half-wave rectifier used to deliver an increased voltage output.

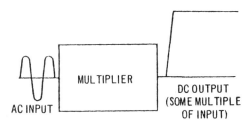

FIGURE 4-14 Block diagram of a voltage multiplier circuit.

HALF-WAVE VOLTAGE DOUBLER

The first voltage multiplier circuit is the half-wave voltage doubler. As the name implies, this circuit gives a dc output that is approximately twice that obtained from the equivalent half-wave rectifier circuit.

Figure 4-15 shows a typical half-wave voltage doubler circuit. While this circuit uses a transformer and the output voltage is positive with respect to ground, it could just as well operate as a negative voltage output by reversing the diodes. The transformer, which may be used to step up secondary voltage or as an isolation transformer, may also be eliminated with the proper choice of circuit elements.

When the top of the transformer secondary in this figure is negative, C_1 will charge through conducting CR_1 to approximately the peak of the secondary voltage. The direction of charge is indicated by the polarity signs. At this time there is no output. On the next alternation, when the top of the transformer secondary is positive with respect to the bottom, C_1 will discharge through the transformer and CR_2, which is now conducting. C_1, which is also in this discharge path, is charged to approximately twice the peak of the secondary voltage because the charge on C_1 is in series with the applied ac and therefore adds to the voltage applied to C_2.

Since C_2 receives only one charge for every cycle of operation, the ripple frequency, as in the half-wave rectifier, is the same as the input frequency. Also, as in the half-wave rectifier, C_2 will discharge slightly between charging cycles, so that filtering is required to smooth the output and provide relatively pure dc.

The procedures for troubleshooting the half-wave voltage doubler are the same as those used for the half-wave rectifier. No output conditions might be caused by a defective transformer, defective rectifiers, an open C_1, or a short-circuited C_2. The low-output condition might be caused by a low input, rectifier aging, or excessive load current (caused by a decrease in load impedance).

The voltage multiplier circuits which follow all have one thing

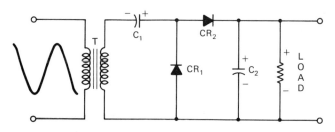

FIGURE 4-15 Half-wave voltage doubler circuit.

in common with the circuit just discussed. They use the charge stored on a capacitor to increase the output voltage. As the voltage across C_1 is added to the input voltage to approximately double the charge applied to C_2, so will the charges on other capacitors add to the charge applied to an input capacitor to double, triple, or quadruple the output voltage.

FULL-WAVE VOLTAGE DOUBLER

The full-wave rectifier circuit can also be adapted to a voltage doubling circuit. Figure 4-16 depicts a basic full-wave voltage doubler circuit. Depending on the circuit application, it may or may not use a power or isolation transformer. The resistor R_S is a surge resistor that is used to limit the charge current and protect the diode. It might not be necessary in some equipment, and when used, it is placed in series with the ac source. Resistors R_1 and R_2 are not necessary for circuit operation but may be used to act as bleeder resistors to discharge their associated capacitors when the circuit is de-energized. When used, they also tend to equalize the voltages across C_1 and C_2.

The circuit operates much the same as the full-wave rectifier previously discussed, with the exception that now two capacitors are employed, each one charging to approximately the peak voltage of the input, adding their charges to provide an output. When point A is positive with respect to point B, C_1 will charge through the conducting diode, CR_1, and the source. It will charge to approximately the peak of the incoming voltage. On the next half cycle of the input, point A is now negative with respect to point B, and CR_2 conducts, charging C_2 in the direction indicated. The voltage across the load will be the total of the voltages across C_1 and C_2. C_1 and C_2 will be equal value capacitors, and R_1 and R_2 will also be equal value resistors. The value of R_S will be small, probably in the 25 to 500-Ω range.

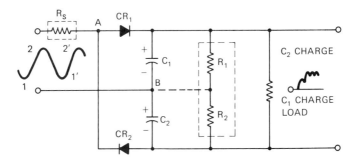

FIGURE 4-16 Basic full-wave voltage doubler.

VOLTAGE TRIPLER

Figure 4-17 depicts a typical voltage tripler circuit with waveforms and circuit operation. Figure 4-17(a) shows the complete circuit. In (b), C_1 is shown charging as CR_2 is conducting. In (c), C_3 is illustrated charging as CR_2 is conducting. Figure 4-17(d) reveals the charge path for C_2 while CR_1 is conducting. In (e), a comparison is made of the input signal and its effects on the voltages felt across C_1, C_2, C_3, and the load. The following explanation uses this figure as the operating device.

Close inspection of part (a) should reveal that removal of CR_3, C_3, R_2, and the load resistor results in the voltage doubler circuit discussed previously. The connection of circuit elements CR_3 and the parallel network C_3 and R_2 to the basic doubler circuit is arranged so that they are in series across the load. The combination provides approximately 3 times more voltage in the output than is felt across the input. Fundamentally, then, this circuit is a combination of a half-wave voltage doubler and a half-wave rectifier circuit arranged so that the output voltage of one circuit is in series with the output voltage of the other.

Figure 4-17(b) shows how C_1 is initially charged. Assume the input is such that CR_2 is conducting. A path for charging current is from the right-hand plate of C_1 through CR_2 and the secondary winding of the transformer to the left-hand plate of C_1. The direction of current is indicated by the arrows.

At the same time that this action is taking place, CR_3 is also forward biased and is conducting, and C_3 is charged with the polarities indicated in (c). The arrows indicate the direction of current. There are now two energized capacitors, each charged to approximately the peak value of the input voltage.

On the next half cycle of the input, the polarities change so that CR_1 is now the conducting diode. Part (d) indicates how capacitor C_1, now in series with the applied voltage, adds its potential to the applied voltage. Capacitor C_2 charges to approximately twice the peak value of the incoming voltage. As can be seen, C_2 and C_3 are in series, and the load resistor is in parallel with this combination. The output voltage then will be the total voltage felt across C_2 and C_3, or approximately 3 times the peak voltage of the input.

Figure 4-17(e) indicates that action taking place using time and the incoming voltage. At time zero (t_0), the ac input is starting on its positive excursion. At this time, the voltage on C_1 and C_3 is increasing. When the input starts to go into its negative excursion, t_1, both C_1 and C_3 start to discharge, and the voltage across C_2 is increasing. The discharge of C_1 adds to the source voltage when charging C_2 so

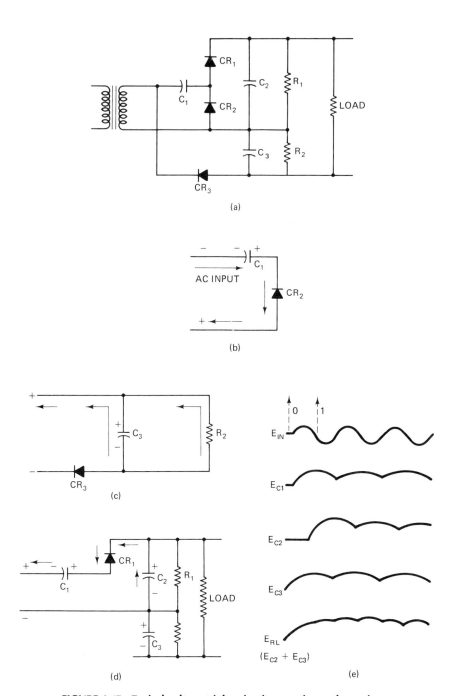

FIGURE 4-17 Typical voltage tripler circuit operation and waveforms.

that the value of E_{C2} is approximately twice the value of the peak value of the input. Since E_{C2} and E_{C3} are in series across the load resistor, the output is their sum.

The charge paths for capacitors C_1, C_2, and C_3 are comparatively low impedance when compared to their discharge paths. Therefore, even though there is some ripple voltage variation in the output voltage, the output voltage will be approximately 3 times the value of the input voltage. The ripple frequency of the output, since capacitors C_2 and C_3 charge on alternate half cycles of the input, is twice that of the input ripple frequency.

Troubleshooting the voltage tripler circuit follows the general practice given for rectifier circuits. The two general categories of failure are no output or low output. For the no-output condition, look for a no-input condition, a lack of applied ac, a defective transformer, or a shorted load circuit. For a low-output condition, check the input voltage. Low input voltage means a correspondingly low output voltage. Low output voltage might also be a result of the rectifier again causing an increased forward resistance or a decreased reverse resistance, any leakage in the capacitors or decrease in their effective capacitor, or an increase in the load current (decrease in load impedance).

VOLTAGE QUADRUPLER

Figure 4-18 shows a typical voltage quadrupler circuit. Essentially, this is two half-wave voltage doubler circuits connected back to back and sharing a common ac input. To show how the voltage quadrupler works, Fig. 4-18 is shown as two voltage doublers. The counterparts of the one circuit are shown as a prime (') in the second circuit. (C_1 in the first circuit is the same as C_1' in the other circuit; CR_1 and CR_1' conduct at the same time, etc.) When the circuit is first turned on, it will be assumed that the top of the secondary winding, point A, is negative with respect to B. At this instance, CR_1 is forward biased and con-

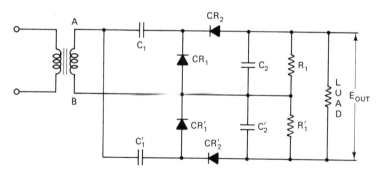

FIGURE 4-18 Voltage quadrupler circuit.

ducts, allowing C_1 to charge. On the next alternation, point B is negative with respect to point A. At this time two things are going to occur:

1. C_1, which was charged to approximately the peak voltage across the secondary winding, will aid the source, and since CR_2 is now conducting, C_2 will be charged to approximately twice the incoming voltage.

2. CR_1' will conduct, charging C_1' to approximately the peak voltage of the input. During the following alternation, C_1' adds to the input, which allows CR_2' to conduct, charging C_2' to twice the input voltage.

When CR_2 conducts, C_1 will aid the input voltage in charging C_2 to approximately twice the peak voltage of the secondary, and CR_2', conducting at the same time, charges C_1'. On the next alternation, CR_1' conducts, and since C_1 is in series with the input, it aids in charging C_2' to twice the peak of the secondary. The voltages across C_2 and C_2' add to provide 4 times the peak secondary voltage in the output.

Voltage multiplier circuits are quite useful in supplying output potentials which are multiples of the rms value of a transformer secondary winding. They are often used when the available winding potential is much lower than the desired dc output. For example, a power transformer with an unused 6-V secondary winding may be used to supply a dc potential of approximately 25 V by using a tripler circuit (4.2 × rms). This could be used to power a separate electronic circuit requiring the 25-V potential. Using standard rectifier configurations, it would be necessary to have a secondary winding with an rms potential of 18-20 V to arrive at the same dc output. Since transformers with secondary windings in this range are relatively rare, the voltage multiplier may be used to facilitate the practicality of electronic circuit building.

5

Thyristors

A thyristor is a solid-state device that has two or more junctions and can be switched between conducting states. It derives its name from a vacuum tube device known as a thyratron. The thyratron is a special type of rectifier which permits control of the amount of energy supplied to a load. Its characteristics are such that a negligible amount of input signal can control thousands of watts of power.

Thyristors perform solid-state switching functions by applying a current pulse of low magnitude to a gate terminal. No mechanical movement occurs, and conduction is controlled by varying the amount of forward bias. Thyristors are typically available as devices which can conduct currents from a low of 1 A to high-powered versions rated at 100 A or more. For this reason, circuits using these devices often control the speed of fairly heavy electric motors, industrial heaters, and other high-powered loads.

SILICON-CONTROLLED RECTIFIER

Perhaps the best known thyristor to electronic enthusiasts is the silicon-controlled rectifier, or SCR, examples of which are pictured in Fig. 5-1. This is a three-junction (*PNPN*) semiconductor device which is normally an open circuit until a proper signal is applied to the gate

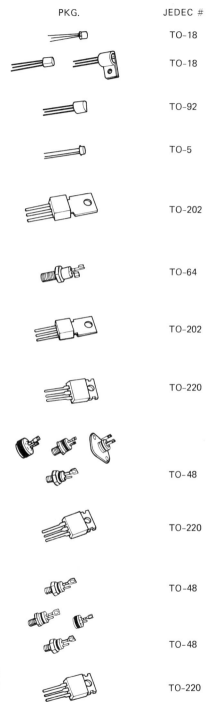

PKG.	JEDEC #
	TO-18
	TO-18
	TO-92
	TO-5
	TO-202
	TO-64
	TO-202
	TO-220
	TO-48
	TO-220
	TO-48
	TO-48
	TO-220

FIGURE 5-1 Common examples of silicon-controlled rectifiers. (Courtesy General Electric.)

Silicon-Controlled Rectifier **67**

element. At this time, it rapidly switches to a conducting state. Figure 5-2 depicts the makeup of the SCR pictorially and schematically.

The following characteristics of the SCR are used to explain the operation of the device:

1. *Forward blocking voltage:* that value of voltage (anode terminal positive with respect to the cathode) that puts the SCR in a forward bias state but which does not switch it to the conducting state.

2. *Breakdown voltage:* the voltage (anode terminal positive with respect to cathode) that causes the SCR to switch to the conductive or *on* state.

3. *Holding current:* that minimum value of anode-cathode current that is required to keep the SCR in conduction. If the anode current drops below this minimum value, the SCR will return to its blocking state.

4. *Reverse blocking region:* that region of SCR operation where the anode terminal is negative with respect to the cathode (reverse bias) but not in avalanche. A light current will flow until the reverse voltage is great enough to cause avalanche (heavy current flow).

5. *Reverse avalanche region:* that region of SCR operation where the maximum reverse voltage (negative anode) has been exceeded and avalanche current flows.

6. *Gate trigger current:* that value of gate current, in the forward direction (gate to cathode), required to trigger an SCR whose anode is positive with respect to its cathode.

7. *Gate trigger voltage:* that value of voltage across the gate to cathode element of an SCR caused by gate trigger current flow. This voltage is measured prior to the SCR reaching a conduction state.

Inspection of Fig. 5-3 indicates that the forward blocking region is largest when gate current is zero. It takes a greater value of forward anode-cathode voltage to cause breakover. As gate current is increased, the forward blocking region is decreased, and the breakover

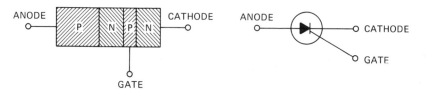

FIGURE 5-2 Pictorial and schematic representation of an SCR.

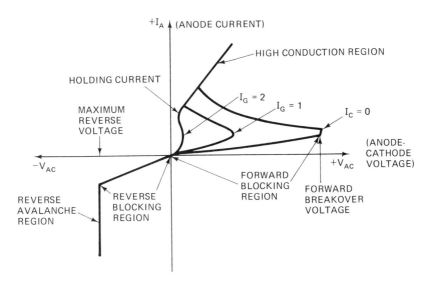

FIGURE 5-3   Voltage-current characteristics of an SCR.

voltage point occurs sooner. When the breakdown voltage value is reached, the gate region of the SCR is effectively eliminated, and the SCR goes into heavy conduction and stays there until anode current drops below the minimum value of holding current. At this time, the SCR reverts to the forward blocking state.

Gate current is an important characteristic of the SCR. With gate current at zero, a high value of anode-cathode voltage in the forward direction would be necessary to cause the SCR to reach the breakover voltage and go into high conduction. As gate current is increased to increase forward bias, the forward blocking region is reduced, and breakover voltage occurs sooner. It is possible to set a value of gate current that would eliminate the forward blocking region entirely, at which time the SCR would perform as a conventional *PN* rectifier.

Once the SCR reaches the high-conduction region, the gate has no control, and the gate area has been effectively eliminated. To regain control, external methods must be applied to the SCR to reduce the flow of anode current. One method is to apply a voltage to the anode that will make the anode negative with respect to the cathode. This will turn the SCR off, putting it back to a forward blocking condition. Another method is to divert enough anode current to some external circuit for a period of time long enough to cause holding current to drop below its minimum value, thereby turning the SCR off. A switch across the anode-cathode terminals, electronically activated or otherwise, will divert the anode current flow. Still another method of turning the SCR off is to cause a heavy reverse current flow from gate to cathode by injecting a reverse voltage. This will cause the gate region

Silicon-Controlled Rectifier   **69**

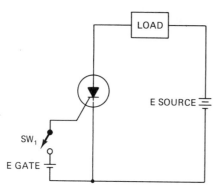

to increase its opposition to anode current flow and allow the gate to regain control of the device.

Figure 5-4 illustrates how the SCR can be used to control a high-power circuit. The breakover voltage with switch 1 open is higher than E source. Therefore, the SCR is not conducting, and there is no current flow through the load. When switch 1 is closed, the breakover voltage is reduced (the forward blocking region is reduced) because of the voltage applied to the gate. The gate voltage causes the SCR to conduct, and current flows through the load. This arrangement enables a low-power line to control a high-power circuit.

The SCR may also be used as a phase control device in various power supply applications. Phase control is a rapid on-off switching process used to connect an ac supply to a load for a controlled fraction of each cycle. By governing the phase angle of an ac wave at which the SCR is allowed to conduct, control of the output of a circuit is accomplished.

A very simple variable-resistance half-wave circuit is shown in Fig. 5-5. This circuit will control the output from essentially zero (full on) to 90 electrical degrees of the anode voltage wave. With the circuit shown here, it is not possible to prevent the SCR from conducting beyond the 90° point, because the supply voltage to the gate and the voltage necessary to trigger the gate to allow the SCR to conduct are in phase. That is, when E source is offering maximum resistance, the

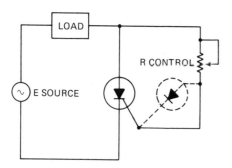

FIGURE 5-5   Simple variable-resistance half-wave phase control.

70   Thyristors

voltage, anode to cathode, is sufficient to cause breakover, and the SCR can be caused to conduct at any point from 0° to 90° by adjusting the control resistor, because the SCR will conduct at the point where gate trigger current is reached. Of course, during the entire negative alternation of the source, the anode-cathode voltage is reversed, and the SCR reverts to a reverse blocking or *off* state. To prevent reverse avalanche, a diode is placed in series with the control resistor and the gate. This diode is shown in Fig. 5-5 enclosed in dotted lines. Figure 5-6 depicts the voltage and current characteristics of the circuit when *R* control is adjusted.

Although it has been shown that the operation of a single-phase

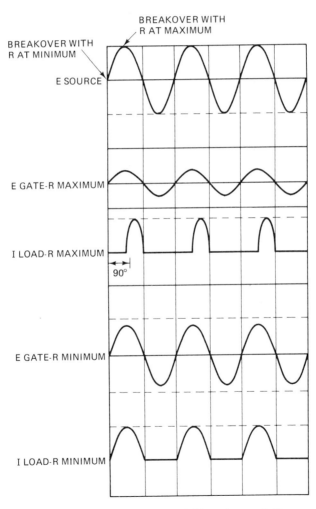

FIGURE 5-6 Characteristics of a simple variable resistance half-wave control circuit.

control circuit allows control of up to 90° of the positive alternation of the input, it is possible to control the entire 360° of the input through the addition of other SCRs, unijunction transistors, and diodes as well as through other methods.

TRIACS

Triac is a General Electric trade name for a thyristor which acts as a full-wave ac silicon switch. The formerly discussed SCR acts as a rectifier when ac voltage is applied between the anode and the cathode (through the load). Therefore, the load always receives a direct-current output. Triacs, on the other hand, may be used to control an ac input and to pass alternating current on to the load.

In effect, a triac is really two reverse-connected silicon-controlled rectifiers, each controlled by a common gate circuit. Figure 5-7 shows how two SCRs may be connected to form the equivalent of a triac.

Like the SCR, the triac has three electrodes and exhibits the same forward blocking, forward conducting, voltage-current characteristics. It does this, however, for either polarity of voltage applied to the main terminals. The breakover voltage of the triac is controlled by application of a small current pulse to the gate electrode. As the current pulse increases in amplitude, the triac breakover point decreases. Figure 5-8 shows a typical triac which physically resembles the silicon-controlled rectifier. Its terminals are designated as gate, main 1, and main 2. The main 2 terminal is the equivalent of the anode of the SCR, while the main 1 terminal compares with the cathode. However, by observing the schematic drawing in Fig. 5-7 once again, it can be seen that main terminal 1 is actually connected to the anode of one of the SCR equivalents and to the cathode of the other simultaneously. The terminal comparison between the two devices just presented has been included from a practical standpoint in that main terminal 1 is connected directly to the load, while main terminal 2 receives the input current.

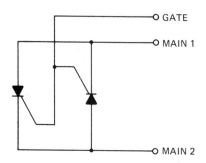

FIGURE 5-7 Two SCRs connected to form the equivalent of a triac.

FIGURE 5-8 Typical triac.

Like silicon-controlled rectifiers, triacs are commonly available to conduct currents in excess of 100 A and with ratings up to approximately 1000 V. They are quite useful for controlling ac motors, lighting sources, and other loads which cannot be operated with direct current. When operating triacs with dc input voltage, the device behaves in the same manner as a single SCR.

DIACS

A diac is another three-layer semiconductor device, but unlike the SCR and triac, it has only two electrodes (compared to their three). Like the triac, it is a bidirectional device which can be switched from the off state to the on state for either polarity of voltage. Diacs are commonly used as trigger devices in conjunction with triacs. This combination especially applies to phase control circuits used for motor speed control, light dimming, etc. Figure 5-9 shows the makeup of the

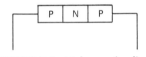

FIGURE 5-9 Makeup of a diac.

diac. This is a *PNP* device and is very similar in construction to a bipolar transistor. It differs from the transistor, however, in that the concentration of impurities at the two junctions (*PN/NP*) is approximately the same, and, of course, there is no base electrode. The result of the equal levels of impurity is a bidirectional switching characteristic.

6

Solid-State
Diode Projects

In this chapter we shall deal specifically with electronic projects using solid-state diodes, rectifiers, silicon-controlled rectifiers, triacs, and optoelectronic devices. Each circuit is presented in schematic diagram form, and a discussion is provided to lead you through the building and checkout process. To be successful in building and operating the following projects, it is necessary for you to have absorbed the information presented in the previous chapters. Experienced electronics assemblers may already be familiar with much of the information, but these discussions provide an excellent review and are highly recommended before actual building is attempted.

You will find that the projects in this chapter range from simple to complex within the context of working with solid-state diodes. Generally, circuits which are composed primarily of these devices are far less complicated than other circuits using transistors, integrated circuits, etc. Some of the projects presented may be built and operated in less than $\frac{1}{2}$h, while others may take several hours or even a weekend to complete.

Regardless of project complexity, do not rush. A rushed project often results in operational failure. Make certain you have all components on hand (including a mounting enclosure if required) before starting. Read the entire discussion surrounding a given project so that you have an idea of what is to be accomplished.

The reader is urged to experiment with these projects, most of which are fairly noncritical. In many instances, substitution of other components will result in circuits which may offer higher power-handling capabilities. Regarding the components specified, I have tried to list those which should be easily obtainable in most general areas. However, situations and availability will vary from location to location, so a good cross-reference catalog may save you many hours of searching for parts that are difficult for you to obtain.

Some circuits will operate from the 115-V household line, so the reader is warned to practice self-preservation at all times. One of the dangers of this household potential lies in the fact that most persons are not all that frightened of a 115-V shock. Given the right circumstances, however, coming in contact with this potential can be deadly. A few of the circuits are designed to multiply the potential of the ac line, and their dc outputs can reach highly lethal potentials. If you have no experience in working with high-voltage circuits, I urge you to seek the assistance and advice of a more experienced individual to guide you through the checkout and alignment procedures.

I think you will find the following circuits to be quite interesting and useful in many different applications. Some will cost you less than $10 and may be equivalent to or even better than commercially manufactured devices costing 10 times this amount or more. The circuits are diversified and will lend themselves nicely to uses around the electronics workbench, in the home or business, and in automobiles. You can even extend this versatility by combining two or more projects. Such hybrids may then be modified to suit individual requirements.

RECTIFIER VOLTAGE CONTROL CIRCUIT

Solid-state rectifiers are most commonly used to change alternating current into direct current. They do this very efficiently and require no power of their own. However, there is a certain amount of voltage drop in any diode owing to its internal resistance to current flow.

The internal voltage drop can be put to excellent use in dc circuits to control output voltage. For example, let's assume you have a logic circuit which requires a 5-V power supply. Assume also that all you have on hand is a 6-V battery. If you knew the current drain of the logic device, you could insert a resistor (of appropriate value) in series with the dc output which would drop 1 V. This would produce an effective potential at the load of 5 V dc. If the logic device drew 1 A, then a 1-Ω resistor would drop 1 V. However, if the device current drain were not constant, problems would develop. As an example, assume that the device draws 1 A during one state and $\frac{1}{2}$ A during another. When current drain is 1 A, 1 V will be dropped, but when the drain decreases to $\frac{1}{2}$A, only $\frac{1}{2}$V would be dropped. During this second state of operation, your supply voltage would increase to 5.5 V dc.

Fortunately, the voltage drop produced by most silicon rectifiers is fairly constant over a wide range of currents. Given the same situation as before, the voltage drop created by an appropriate silicon rectifier would be much more constant for the two values of current drain.

Figure 6-1 shows a simple circuit which uses three silicon diodes, each of which produces an approximate drop of 1 V. I used the SK9091/177 silicon rectifier, which is rated at 200 PRV with an average forward current maximum of 200 mA. This type of diode just happened to be on hand, and most junk box types will do as well. You might consult the manufacturer's specifications if you intend to purchase the diodes for this circuit in order to choose units which give you the forward voltage drop needed. These are approximate values and can fluctuate from unit to unit. Typical drops range from .8 to 1.5 V dc.

Looking at the circuit, it can be seen that three rectifiers are wired in series, with a switch contact brought off each. This provides control of output voltage in steps equal to the forward voltage drop of each diode combined. For example, if the switch is positioned at the no-contact point (NC), all three rectifiers will be in the circuit, so the total voltage drop will be the sum of the forward voltage drop in all three. By moving the switch to the next position, the first diode is removed from the circuit, and the voltage drop is equal to the sum of D_2 and D_3. In the next position, only the single diode D_3 is in the circuit. In the last position, all diodes are effectively removed, giving you the full potential of the battery.

I used a four-position rotary switch for my circuit, with the contacts rated at 500 mA. Maximum current drain was to be no more than 180 mA, so the switch and diode all operated well within their

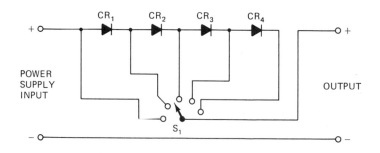

CR$_1$-CR$_4$: 50 PIV, 2 A

S$_1$: 5-POSITION ROTARY SWITCH, 1-A CONTACTS

FIGURE 6-1   Rectifier voltage control circuit.

76 Solid-State Diode Projects

maximum ratings. To make the circuit as simple as possible from a construction standpoint, the rectifiers were wired directly to the S_1 contacts. The outputs from D_3 and the negative battery terminal were connected directly to a two-terminal strip. A small plastic enclosure was used to house the circuit and was drilled to accept the shaft of S_1. It will be necessary to mark the four switch positions to indicate the amount of voltage drop for each. The battery is installed in an appropriate holder inside the compartment. I used mine with a 9-V transistor radio battery, but any other type will work as long as its output voltage does not exceed the rating of the silicon rectifiers.

To test this circuit, connect an accurate dc voltmeter across the output terminals. The metering scale should be capable of reading the full output potential of B_1. Now, set S_1 to the no-contact position and note the reading. This should be identical to the battery voltage. Now, rotate S_1 through all its positions, noting the voltage drop each time. Write these figures down on a nearby notepad, and when you're finished, examine the results. You should receive a lower output voltage reading as you advance through the switch positions. If the voltage drops do not suit your needs, then try substituting different diodes. Remember, two identical diodes from the same manufacturer may induce slightly different voltage drops. You can even try connecting two similar diodes in parallel to significantly decrease the drop in that particular switching stage. This is where experimentation and many substitutions are necessary to arrive at the voltage drop steps that you need for operation of various circuits. Once you have chosen the correct components, the four switch positions can be marked with the output voltage presented by each. If you wish to raise or lower the overall output of the supply, simply change to a different battery. The voltage drops induced by each stage will still be about the same. For instance, if when using a 6-V battery position number 2 gives you an output of 5 V (a 1-V drop), then when using a 12-V battery, you will still get the 1-V drop for an output of 11 V dc.

The circuit presented here uses only three series diodes, but you can use as many as you want to obtain the voltage steps needed. Make certain the rectifier ratings reflect battery voltage and the amount of current you wish to draw. This project allows for maximum current output of 200 mA, but 1-A rectifiers would increase the maximum output 5 times. Also make certain that the contacts of S_1 are rated to withstand the maximum current drain.

All in all, I think you will find this to be a very useful circuit, especially for operating electronic projects whose outputs can be controlled by raising or lowering the input voltage. By using the required number of series rectifiers, you can build a variable power supply which will produce an output of from 1.5 to 12 V dc, assuming the use of a 12-V battery. The term variable supply is not exactly accurate here, as a true variable circuit will allow for the linear adjustment of voltage values. This circuit makes the adjustment in increments, but when set up properly, it is almost as versatile as an expensive linearly variable dc power supply.

AC CONTROL CIRCUIT

The previous project involved a method of lowering the value of dc voltage by switching diode rectifiers in and out of a line. The output from this circuit is always direct current, even if the input should be alternating current. However, this same method may be used for controlling ac output voltage. The circuit is shown in Fig. 6-2 and is similar to the previous project, with the exception that cross-connected rectifiers have been used. At first glance, this circuit may look a bit strange, but remember the purpose is to control an alternating current. There are three switching positions, each of which will bring about a decrease in voltage, owing to the internal resistance of the rectifiers.

To explain this circuit, it is necessary once again to discuss the operation of a basic rectifier. When positive-going current is applied at the anode of a rectifier, it becomes forward biased and conducts. When the anode swings to negative, the rectifier is reverse biased and ceases to conduct. In this circuit, however, pairs of rectifiers are used in reverse-connected fashion to allow for current of changing polarities to always be passed. Let's assume that only the first stage of this circuit consisting of D_1 and D_2 is actually in the ac line. During one polarity swing, D_1 will be forward biased and will conduct. At the same time, D_2 will be reverse biased and will not conduct. The voltage drop incurred is that of only a single diode in the pair. During the next half cycle, polarity will reverse and so will the conducting

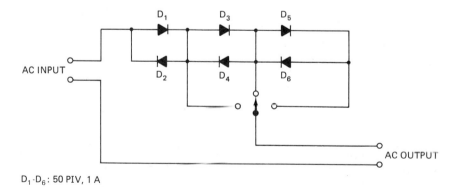

D_1-D_6: 50 PIV, 1 A

FIGURE 6-2 Ac-controlled circuit using reverse-connected rectifiers.

states of the diode. D_1 conducts during the positive swing, while D_2 conducts during the negative portion of the cycle. Both diodes are matched units, so the total voltage drop at the ac output will be equivalent to the voltage drop across a single diode.

The remaining two stages allow for further voltage drops, and you may incorporate as many as desirable for your individual requirements. Admittedly, this circuit would be impractical if large changes in ac voltage value are necessary. Many, many diode pairs would be required to effect such a change. This circuit will be most applicable at the low-voltage secondary windings of some small power transformers and where it may be desirable to alter the ac output by a few volts. Using the components shown, the circuit may be used with ac inputs of up to 30 V and with a maximum ac current drain of approximately 800 mA. This applies to single-stage operation only. Since the stages are effectively wired in series, the total voltage rating of each component is added by the number of components in each series string (as are the voltage drops). Using all three stages in series, the effective PIV rating is 150 V. Naturally, you may use rectifiers rated at much higher peak inverse voltages and forward current ratings to control higher ac values.

The circuit may be built in much the same manner as the previous one. Just make certain that each diode pair is reverse connected (the anode of one diode connected to the cathode of the other). If this is not done, you will end up with a pulsating dc output and the rough equivalent of the former project.

TWO-POSITION ILLUMINATION SWITCH

Incandescent lights, the kind nearly every home has, will operate from both ac and dc, and this attribute can be taken advantage of in designing a simple circuit which will allow you to instantly halve lamp illumination at the flick of a switch. During full illumination, the electric light will be operating at the full 115 V ac potential. When at half illumination, the light will be receiving a dc input of approximately 55 V.

The circuit is shown in Fig. 6-3 and consists of a single diode and an SPST switch. All the switch does is short out the diode when full illumination is desired. The ac current flow will then pass through the closed switch contacts. When S_1 is opened, the ac circuit is broken, and direct current flows through the diode and the lamp. Since this is a half-wave rectifier, only half of the ac sine cycle will be rectified, and the former rms value will be halved. The output from this rectifier circuit is unfiltered, so pulsating dc will be the result, and the lamp will flicker at the dc pulse rate. Do not attempt to install an

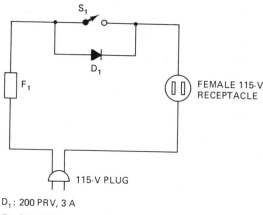

D₁ : 200 PRV, 3 A

D_1 : 200 PRV, 3 A
F_1 : 2 A FUSE
S_1 : SPST, 3 A

FIGURE 6-3 Two-position illumination control.

electrolytic capacitor across the output of the rectifier, as this will actually increase the voltage to a point above the original rms value. Also, when S_1 is closed, ac would be placed across the electrolytic capacitor, creating a potential fire hazard.

I designed my circuit for outboard use. A small aluminum box was cut to accept a female 115-V receptacle. The rectifier was wired directly to one of the receptacle contacts, as was one of the switch leads. The remaining switch lead was attached to the opposite rectifier lead and also connected at this point to one side of the 115-V power line. The remaining conductor in the line cord was attached directly to the remaining receptacle contact.

This circuit is designed for loads up to 200 W. A 3-A diode is slightly overrated for this application, which is desirable. A 2-A fuse is installed at the input to the circuit and will open if loads requiring more than 200 W are inadvertently connected. Examine your wiring very carefully and be sure to use a grounded power plug and cable. The ground connection is made at the aluminum enclosure. The ground from the female receptacle is also made at the same point. Make certain there is no short circuit between the ac line, the output from the diode, and the aluminum box.

To test the circuit, attach the line cord from the lamp to the receptacle and plug the line cord from this project into a 115 V receptacle. With the switch closed, the lamp should operate normally. When you open the switch, the lamp output should be cut by half or even more. Make certain S_1 is rated to pass at least 3 A. Some miniature switches are rated for a maximum current flow of 1 A and can be a fire hazard if used in this circuit. *Caution:* When S_1 is open, the output from this circuit is pulsating dc. Use only incandescent lamps as loads for this circuit. If you should connect fluorescent lamps or other ac-only devices to the output, severe damage to these loads can occur. This is especially true of electronic circuits which utilize transformers. Connecting dc to the primary of a transformer places a short circuit across the diode output and will destroy it. You might also damage the electronic load, as a high amount of voltage could be present at the secondary output for a fraction of a second.

TWO-STATE LIGHT SWITCH-DIMMER

The circuit shown in Fig. 6-4 accomplishes much the same effect as the previous project, except the output to the 115-V receptacle is always alternating current (ac). To accomplish this, a triac has been used, which is actually two silicon-controlled rectifiers combined. The device will conduct current in either direction and is used for ac control. This circuit goes a bit further, however, and provides a means of linearly dimming an incandescent lamp as well as being able to cut the illumination output in half.

This circuit is designed to handle loads of up to 200 W and should be installed in a grounded aluminum box. The ground is made to the ac service by means of the third plug pin. Actually, you can design this circuit for more high-powered operations by using a different triac. The RCA unit specified will handle a maximum of 2.5 A, which amounts to over 280 W of power, but the 200-W maximum is maintained for device safety.

You can install the triac and D_1 on a small section of perforated

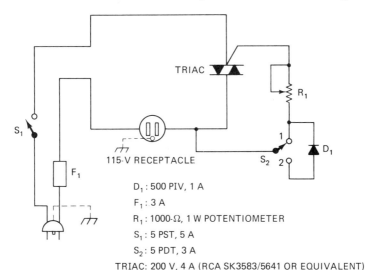

D$_1$: 500 PIV, 1 A

F$_1$: 3 A

R$_1$: 1000-Ω, 1 W POTENTIOMETER

S$_1$: 5 PST, 5 A

S$_2$: 5 PDT, 3 A

TRIAC: 200 V, 4 A (RCA SK3583/5641 OR EQUIVALENT)

FIGURE 6-4 Two-state light switch-dimmer.

circuit board or use a terminal strip for the same purposes. The latter arrangement will save some space. R_1, S_1, S_2, and the 115-V receptacle are installed through the aluminum case. You may also wish to install a through-case fuseholder for F_1 or use an in-line type of holder.

The operation of this circuit is quite simple. When S_2 is in the No. 1 switch position, R_1 is adjusted until the triac is triggered, passing alternating current to the 115-V receptacle. You can adjust R_1 with the load connected to create a dimming effect as the voltage is raised and lowered.

When S_2 is switched to the No. 2 position, D_1 is brought into the circuit. This causes the SCR to be triggered only on alternate half cycles, and the voltage at the receptacle is halved. This makes the circuit more versatile than the previous one in that many functions are provided and the output is alternating current.

As a safety measure, I installed a clip-on heat sink to the triac case. If you design this circuit for high-power operation, you will probably need to install a fairly large finned heat sink to allow the triac to cool properly. With S_2 in the No. 1 position and a power transformer connected to the receptacle, you can use R_1 to vary the primary input potential, which will allow you to lower the secondary voltage. When S_2 is in the No. 2 position, the output at the receptacle is still alternating current. The diode does perform a rectifying function but only between the gate and one side of the triac. It does not rectify the output to the receptacle.

Before testing this circuit, reexamine your wiring to make certain there are no shorts between the 115-V line and the case. Also, make certain your case is grounded to the appropriate plug pin through the three-wire cable. While this circuit was set up for 115-V ac operation, it can be modified for 230-V operation by substituting an RCA SK3506/5642 for the triac specified. The latter component will operate at up to 400 V ac. If you make this substitution, your available output power at the receptacle is doubled, because 2 A may still be drawn. *Caution:* The metal case of the triac will be at the power line potential, so make certain it does not come in contact with the aluminum enclosure. Alternately, you may use a plastic enclosure, but make certain the line plug and 115-V receptacle are equipped with ground pins.

PROTECTION CIRCUITS

Anyone who has had the misfortune of connecting an expensive electronic device to a dc power supply with the positive and negative leads reversed knows the disasters that can occur through polarity mismatch. When the positive lead is inadvertently connected to the negative supply output and the negative lead connected to positive, internal solid-state components within the load can be instantly destroyed. To avoid such disasters, many manufacturers elect to protect their equipment by using simple diode circuits. Many others do not, however, so the circuits contained here may be quite important as additions to your current dc power equipment.

Figure 6-5 shows one of the simplest forms of adding diode protection to an existing piece of equipment. A diode will conduct current in only one direction. This property is taken advantage of in this circuit, which contains a diode rectifier in the positive input lead from the power supply. The diode must be connected with the anode and cathode wired as shown. Now, current of a positive polarity is allowed to flow through the load. Should you switch the power supply input leads, the diode is reverse biased, and no power whatsoever is connected to the load. You can alter this circuit by installing the diode in the negative supply lead, but in this application this component is reversed. Either way, the installation of this circuit at the output of a power supply or at the input to the load device will prevent component damage through polarity reversal.

This circuit has one drawback. The diode is connected in series with the power supply, and current is drawn through the device. All diodes will drop a certain amount of supply voltage due to their internal resistance. Therefore, slightly less than the full voltage potential is delivered to the load. Most silicon rectifiers drop little more than 1 V, but this can have an effect on some electronic loads, such as citizens band transceivers. The result is a very slight drop in output power while transmitting. From a practical standpoint, the $\frac{1}{2}$-W or so decrease will not be noticed in on-the-air operations, but in devices which are extremely critical as to input voltage, the addition of this circuit may create problems. D_1 is chosen based on the power supply voltage and the current drawn by the load. Components rated at 50 PRV will be adequate for all automotive operations (using the automotive electrical system). If the load draws 1 A, play it safe and use a rectifier rated at 2 A. This will give you the protection needed upon initial activation of the load, when high peak currents may be drawn.

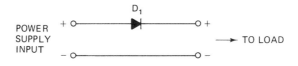

D_1 : SILICON RECTIFIER RATED TO HANDLE POWER
SUPPLY VOLTAGE AND LOAD CURRENT

FIGURE 6-5 Series diode protection circuit.

Owing to the inherent voltage which occurs anytime a rectifier is installed in series with the power supply input to a device, most manufacturers of citizens band equipment elect to shunt the rectifier across the power supply input as shown in Fig. 6-6. This is a self-destruct circuit in that when a reversed polarity condition occurs, the diode conducts, blowing the series fuse and often destroying itself almost simultaneously. Sometimes the diode will survive, but this is extremely rare.

By looking at the circuit, it can be seen that when the power supply input is directly connected, the diode is reverse biased so no current flows. However, should a reversal occur, the diode then becomes forward biased and conducts. This creates a short circuit across the power supply input to the electronic device and ahead of the device circuitry. The fuse is rated to withstand normal operation, but when the diode conducts, the fuse limitations are exceeded, and it opens up. The electronic device is protected, but unlike the previous circuit, it is necessary to replace the fuse and D_1 after each reversal. The redeeming feature of this circuit lies in the fact that the diode is not installed in series with the power supply and does not drop voltage under normal operating conditions. The circuit may be thought of as inactive until the reversal occurs. It very effectively prevents serious internal damage to the electronic device, but it's not 100% foolproof.

One might ask why the diode is destroyed during a reversal when its main purpose is to blow the fuse. The fact of the matter is that the tiny junction within the diode is a better fuse than the fuse itself. By the time sufficient current has been conducted through the diode to open the fuse, the junction is already irreparably damaged. On rare occasions, the diode can destroy itself before the fuse has time to blow, and reverse current is still fed to the electronic circuit. Occasionally, the diode will be destroyed, the fuse opened, and the electronic circuit still damaged. The reason for this lies in the time lag which occurs between the time reverse current is connected, the diode conducts, and the fuse blows. By using this circuit, a reverse connection at the power supply input causes reverse current to be momentarily passed to the electronic load. The gamble here is that the diode will blow the fuse before the solid-state components in the load are damaged. Often, the system works; about as often, however, it does not. In my opinion, this circuit is better than no protection at

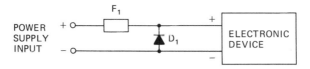

FIGURE 6-6 Parallel diode protection circuit.

all, but it's still not as good as the previous one which uses the series diode.

The two preceding circuits have accomplished one thing. When a polarity reversal occurs, they prevent the load from receiving any current at all (overlooking the time lag of a few milliseconds in the second circuit). Wouldn't it be nice to have a circuit at the input to your expensive transceiver which would automatically switch the power supply input to the correct polarity even when a reversal has occurred? Such a circuit does exist, and it's one you're very familiar with. It's called a full-wave bridge rectifier. When ac input is connected to a full-wave bridge rectifier, one terminal is automatically at a positive potential, while the other is negative. Remember, alternating current is constantly reversing polarity. During one-half of the ac cycle, one of the input terminals is positive while the other is negative. During the other half of the cycle, the input polarities are reversed. What this means is regardless of what the input polarity is, the two dc output terminals will always remain at their fixed polarity states.

Of course, you won't be operating your transceiver or other electronic device with an ac input but rather with direct current. This is no problem. When a dc input is connected to the input of a full-wave bridge rectifier, the positive and negative output terminals will still be positive and negative, regardless of the polarity of the input leads. Technically, the first protection circuit discussed was a half-wave rectifier, and so was the second one, but in a destructive vein.

Figure 6-7 shows a full-wave bridge protection circuit which may be used with any dc-driven device. This is identical to a circuit you would build for rectification purposes, but in this case rectification has taken place before input terminals A and B are accessed. To illustrate how this circuit operates, assume that the positive power supply output lead is connected to terminal A and the negative one to B. By using this configuration, diode D_1 is forward biased and con-

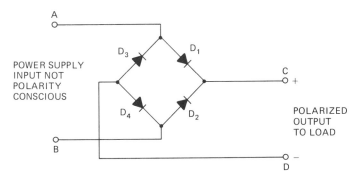

FIGURE 6-7 Bridge rectifier protection circuit.

ducts current to the positive output terminal (*C*). Likewise, diode D_4 is forward biased by the negative input from *B* and conducts current of a negative polarity to terminal *D*. D_2 and D_4 are both reverse biased and do not conduct any current.

Now let's reverse the power supply connections with the negative lead attached to *A* and the positive one to *B*. D_2 is now forward biased and conducts current of a positive nature to terminal *C*. D_3 is forward biased and conducts negative-going current to terminal *D*. In the latter instance, D_1 and D_4 are reverse biased and do not conduct at all.

Note that in both configurations the positive output was always at terminal *C*, while the negative output was at terminal *D*. It makes no difference whatsoever (polarity-wise) how the power supply input is connected. Either way, the output to the load will remain positive at *C* and negative at *D*. These two outputs will be connected to the positive and negative load inputs, respectively. Make sure you don't reverse the output connections to the load. The results of this would definitely be disastrous, since no matter how you connected the input from the power supply, the current to the load would always be reverse connected.

The last circuit is the one which I use most often in the circuits I wish to protect from a possible current reversal. Instead of using four discrete diodes, I have found that the packaged bridge rectifiers require far less mounting space and are easier to install within the enclosure of the existing electronic device. For 12-V automotive operation, 50-PIV diodes or rectifier packages are more than adequate. Current ratings of the devices are determined by the current drain of the load.

This circuit may sound quite ideal, but there is one drawback. As was the case with the first protection circuit, this one uses series diodes. Here, two diodes are placed in series with the dc power supply output, and a voltage drop to the load is the result. The drop is more severe here because two diodes are connected instead of just one. Using this circuit at 12 V dc will produce a supply drop to the load of about 2 V. Most electronic equipment that is designed to be operated from the automotive electrical system will work well with input voltage ranging from 11 to 15 V dc. There are some exceptions, but remember that the automotive electrical system supplies only 12 V dc when the motor is not running and nearly 14 V when it is. If this circuit is installed, your electronic equipment will still be getting approximately 21 V dc when the motor is running. I have used this circuit in many different pieces of automotive, entertainment, and communications equipment and am completely satisfied with the overall performance.

Any of the circuits discussed here will go a long way toward preventing expensive component damage brought on by a power supply reversal. All equipment which you build at home should be fitted with some type of protective circuit. Examine any commercial equipment to see if protection is provided, and if not, install one of these three circuits to assure continued operation.

CLAMPING DIODE PROTECTION

A few decades ago, most power switching circuits were mechanical in nature and used relays or standard switches to accomplish power on-off functions. Today this is not always true. Often a transistor or silicon-controlled rectifier is used for these purposes. For example, a relay may be placed in series with the collector of the transistor and its power source. When the transistor is in the nonconducting state, no current is passed to ground, and the relay is not activated. When a small amount of signal is fed to the base of the transistor, however, it becomes forward biased and conducts. This allows current to flow through the relay coil and activates the switching contacts. This example explains how a solid-state switch (the transistor) is used to trigger an electromechanical switch (the relay) by going into the conduction state.

A relay of the electromechanical type contains an internal inductor or coil, which is really an electromagnet. Like all coils, it presents a high amount of lumped inductance. The same is true of motors, chokes, and other inductor devices. When the transistor conducts, electrons move through the coil. Unfortunately, they move through with such force that they don't want to stop, even after the transistor has returned to the nonconducting or off state. When the transistor turns off, current is suddenly blocked. Due to the inductive kick from the coil, the electrons keep coming and build up to a high-voltage value at the collector electrode. While the relay may be designed to operate at 12 V dc, the electron kick can cause the value to build to many times this level. A high buildup can exceed the maximum ratings of the transistor, and current can break through the transistor and damage or destroy it.

Figure 6-8 shows a simple transistor switch used to activate an electromechanical relay. Note that the positive current source is connected through the relay coil and to the transistor collector. The emitter is grounded. For the relay to activate, current must be allowed to flow through the coil, through the transistor, and finally to ground. (Actually, the exact reverse is true in that current flows from ground to the positive source, but the same basic operating principles apply.) The transistor is either on or off. Its operational state is controlled by the basic circuit.

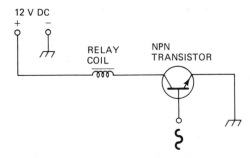

FIGURE 6-8 Simple circuit using a transistor to switch current through a relay coil.

Figure 6-9 shows the same circuit with the addition of a single diode that is connected in parallel with the relay coil. Note that the diode is normally reverse biased or will be if the coil is removed from the circuit. The cathode of the diode is connected to the positive power terminal, while the anode is connected to the opposite side of the relay coil. The diode will not allow electrons from the power supply to bypass the coil and be fed directly to the transistor. It will allow electrons to bypass the coil when current flows in the opposite direction. The damage occurs when the inductive kick voltage value exceeds that of the power supply (in this case, 12 V). When the voltage at the collector input exceeds the power supply voltage, the diode conducts (is forward biased) and effectively drains the electrons away from the transistor. When used in this manner, the diode is called a clamp. Here the voltage is clamped at 12 V dc or less.

Almost any silicon diode can be used for clamping purposes. Just make sure its PRV rating is considerably higher than the power supply voltage. In most instances, I use a 1000-PRV 1-A diode, since these are inexpensive and quite easy to find. For a circuit powered from 12 V dc, a 50-PRV or 100-PRV component should be fine, but this will depend on the inductance of the coil.

Again, make certain the diode is connected across the inductor as shown in the schematic drawing. This circuit uses an NPN transistor, which requires a positive potential at its collector. If a PNP transistor were used, the collector would be connected to a negative potential, and it would be necessary to reverse the polarity of the diode.

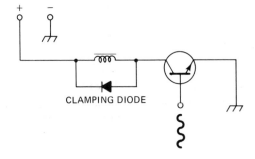

FIGURE 6-9 Single diode connected in parallel with the relay coil protects the switching transistor from voltage pileup.

I think you will find this clamping circuit to be ideal for most transistor switching applications using inductive devices. A 50-cent diode can go a long way toward preventing burnout of an expensive transistor.

ZENER DIODE OVERVOLTAGE PROTECTION

Some electronic circuits may be operated at near their maximum input potentials. For example, if a device uses a transistor or integrated circuit which must not be operated at over 12 V dc and a supply is used which is supposed to provide exactly 12 V dc, it can be safely said that this is the maximum supply voltage or the value which must not be exceeded. Unfortunately, conditions can be generated within any dc power supply, including storage batteries, whereby the maximum output voltage can rise. Such occurrences are especially prevalent when the device under power is initially activated. This can cause the output from the power supply to increase tremendously (but only for small fractions of a second), and this most often occurs when the power supply is turned on with the device. Such instances may be enough to "pop" an expensive solid-state component.

The circuit shown in Fig. 6-10 uses a zener diode to protect the circuit from overvoltage occurrences. The zener diode is chosen to present a value which is slightly higher than the maximum operating potential. For example, if your device is powered from a 9-V battery, a 9.1-V zener diode would conduct when the supply potential reaches 9.1 V, one-tenth of 1 V higher than the maximum operating potential. The zener does no conducting whatsoever as long as the voltage is below this value, but when its *zener knee* (in this case, 9.1 V dc) is exceeded, the device conducts heavily. The increased current drain causes a voltage drop within the power supply, bringing the value down below the conducting state. The zener then switches off. This is exactly the way a zener diode voltage regulator works, but a series resistor is included in this mode of operation. As shown, the zener diode depends on the internal resistance of the power supply to drop the voltage. If the internal resistance is not great enough, the zener will be destroyed.

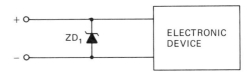

FIGURE 6-10 Zener diode circuit to protect from power supply overvoltage.

ZD$_1$: 1-W ZENER DIODE, RATED AT SLIGHTLY MORE THAN DEVICE OPERATING VOLTAGE.

It's quite easy to protect delicate electronic equipment by using the zener diode circuit shown. In most instances, the single component can be mounted within the enclosure of the equipment it is there to protect. Usually this circuit will be used to prevent a serious overvoltage condition. For instance, a circuit which is operated at 12 V dc will probably do just fine at 1 or 2 V in excess of this value. So a 15-V zener might be chosen to avoid a serious overvoltage condition, which might be the result of a suddenly defective or erratic dc power supply.

Zener diodes are available in common values such as 6, 9.1, 12, 15, and 18 V dc. These are the kinds you will most likely find in a local hobby store. However, you can order a zener diode in almost any value imaginable from the major solid-state component manufacturers. RCA lists them in values of from 2.4 to 200 V dc, with many, many small step increments in between. For example, if you wanted to protect a circuit which was to be operated at a nominal 12 V dc, you could choose a zener rated at 12.8, 13, or 14 V dc. When using power supplies or batteries with low internal resistances, it might be best to use a 5-W zener, which you probably won't find locally but can order with little difficulty. Hopefully, the zener will never have to conduct, but if it does, you can be certain that its presence is definitely needed to protect the delicate (and sometimes expensive) solid-state components within the circuit.

ANOTHER OVERVOLTAGE PROTECTION CIRCUIT

If you would prefer to go the electromechanical route in providing overvoltage protection, the circuit shown in Fig. 6-11 should interest you. This circuit is designed to be attached to any existing power supply, although the components specified were designed to operate at a 12-V output. A zener diode which is rated at 13 V dc is connected to the positive output terminal and in series with a 12-V latching relay whose negative terminal is connected to the negative power supply output. Its normally closed switch contacts are in series with one leg of the power line. As long as the power supply output voltage is kept below the 13-V level, the zener and relay are not activated. When this potential is reached, however, the zener conducts, passing current through the relay coil. Again, its contacts are normally closed, but when the relay is energized, they open and disconnect primary power to the supply. It is not absolutely necessary to use a latching relay, but it's highly impractical to do otherwise. When a latching relay is tripped, its contacts will remain in the energized state (after engaging) regardless of whether or not the coil continues to be energized. By using this circuit, an overvoltage situation will switch the

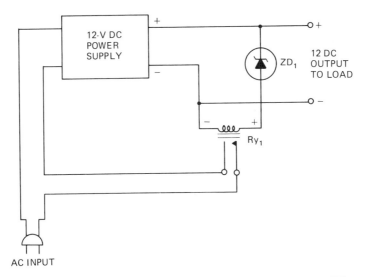

AC INPUT

Ry_1: 12-V MINIATURE LATCHING RELAY NORMALLY CLOSED CONTACTS
ZD_1: 13-V, 1-W ZENER DIODE

FIGURE 6-11 Electromechanical overvoltage protection circuit.

supply off and keep it off until the relay is manually reset. If you should use a nonlatching relay, an overvoltage situation would remove primary power, but you must remember that this also removes dc output power. In other words, this immediately corrects the overvoltage situation, and since the line cord is still connected to the ac outlet, the power supply will be immediately reenergized. If the overvoltage condition still exists, the cycle will be repeated again and again. A well-designed dc power supply should not produce excessive voltage, except during conditions where a malfunction such as a damaged component occurs. When the power supply is switched off by this protective circuit, this is usually a sign that repairs are needed. Therefore, the circuit should be given a thorough going over before it is operated again.

BUILDING A TRIAC

While neither component is especially rare, one usually sees more silicon-controlled rectifiers than triacs. This is particularly true in hobby stores, where you may find a large assortment of SCRs but only one or two types of triacs. Certainly, you can order a triac of almost any specification from an electronic component catalog, but delivery can sometimes take 2 weeks or so.

When you need to obtain a triac quickly, perhaps the best thing to do is to build one yourself. A triac is merely two reverse parallel-connected silicon-controlled rectifiers. True, the triacs you obtain commercially handle this configuration on a single chip of silicon, but you won't notice any lack of efficiency by using two discrete components. Figure 6-12 shows the basic circuit. No component specifications are given, since any two identical SCRs will work.

The anode of one triac is connected to the cathode of the other. The same is true of the remaining anode and cathode leads. The gate leads are also wired in parallel. You now have a triac. If each SCR was rated at 200 PRV and 3 A of forward current, then the combination will have identical ratings. This circuit may be connected in place of any triac included in any of the circuits in this chapter. It may be necessary to alter the value of the gate circuit resistor in some applications, but since this is often a variable type, this presents few problems.

Previous discussions in this book have dealt with equalization circuits attached to parallel-connected rectifiers. Similar protection circuits are necessary when silicon-controlled rectifiers are connected in parallel for increased current gains. This, however, does not apply to the reverse parallel connection of SCRs as presented in this project. Current will flow through only one component at any time. One of the SCRs will be forward biased during one-half of the ac cycle, while the other is reverse biased. During the next half of the cycle, the components switch modes of operation. In most ways, the two components act independently of each other, with each conducting during one-half of the cycle. For this reason, no external equalization resistors are required.

The circuit as shown may also be used with a dc input to control dc loads, since only one of the SCRs will be conducting. However, a single SCR can also be used with an ac input to control dc loads due to the rectification that takes place. This circuit will not rectify, so

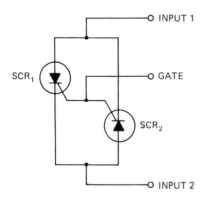

SCR₁-SCR₂: IDENTICAL SILICON-CONTROLLED RECTIFIERS

FIGURE 6-12 Triac formed by two silicon-controlled rectifiers in reverse parallel.

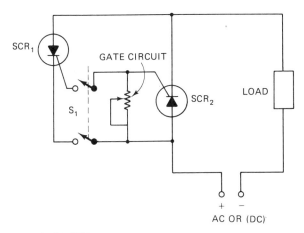

SCR₁

GATE CIRCUIT

SCR₂

LOAD

S₁

+ −
AC OR (DC)

S₁ : DPST SWITCH

FIGURE 6-13 Switching arrangement allowing for ac or dc load control.

if you have an ac input, an ac load must be connected. With a dc input, the load must be designed to receive direct current.

The schematic shown in Fig. 6-13 is a slight modification of the previous one and uses a double-pole/single-throw switch to allow for the control of ac or dc loads with an ac or dc input. When the switch is opened, SCR₁ is removed from the circuit, leaving only SCR₂. An ac input with the switch in this position will be rectified, and dc current will be passed to the load. When the switch is closed, SCR₁ is brought into the circuit, forming a triac which will pass ac current to the load (assuming an ac input). This is quite a handy circuit to have around the electronic workbench, as it offers control of ac or dc loads from a single circuit merely by flipping the switch to the correct position. You must be extremely cautious when using this circuit in order to be certain of delivering the correct current to the load. If you should inadvertently leave the switch in the dc position while connected to an ac load, severe damage to the load may result from the dc input.

For high-powered circuits, it will be necessary to equip each SCR with a separate heat sink. If you use an exceptionally large finned sink, you may be able to mount both components here, but in most instances, two separate sinks will provide the greatest thermal protection.

STROBEFLASH SLAVE ADAPTER

In photographic work, it is often desirable when using an electronic strobe flash to use a remote or *slave* flash synchronized with the master unit. This can involve situations where one flash unit is not adequate to light the entire subject. A slave flash unit is installed at a different angle to the subject and is automatically fired at the same time as the master flash unit. This can be done using hookup wiring between the camera and the two strobes, but this can be awkward and may greatly limit the photographer.

The circuit shown in Fig. 6-14 is self-contained and may be mounted at the slave unit. The flash from the master unit activates this slave circuit, which uses a phototransistor in the gate circuit of a silicon-controlled rectifier. When the light burst is present at the Q_1 lens, the phototransistor conducts, and the 9-V battery supplies current to the SCR gate circuit through R_1. The dc power supply for the slave unit is connected in series with the anode and cathode of the silicon-controlled rectifier and supplies current directly to the slave when the SCR is conducting. Any SCR will work with this circuit as long as it is rated to handle the full current flow of the strobe power supply. It may be necessary to readjust R_1, however, to bring about proper firing.

The phototransistor used in this circuit is cut off until the flash occurs. This is due to the relatively low resistance of the RF choke (L_1), even under high ambient light conditions. When a fast-rising pulse of light strikes the base region of this device, L_1 acts as a very high impedance, and the transistor is biased into conduction. When this occurs, a signal is applied to the SCR gate. The SCR acts as a solid-state relay, turning on the strobeflash unit.

You can construct this circuit on perf board, or you may use a six-contact terminal strip for the same purpose. I used perforated circuit board and mounted the entire circuit in a small plastic en-

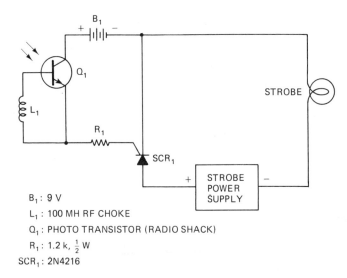

B$_1$: 9 V
L$_1$: 100 MH RF CHOKE
Q$_1$: PHOTO TRANSISTOR (RADIO SHACK)
R$_1$: 1.2 k, $\frac{1}{2}$ W
SCR$_1$: 2N4216

FIGURE 6-14 Strobeflash adapter circuit.

closure which was drilled to accept the phototransistor. The lens of this device must be exposed to the master unit. The output from the SCR was then connected in series with the dc power supply of the slave, which remains active at all times.

To test the circuit, simply activate the slave power supply and then flash the master unit. The slave should flash in sync. If not, check your connections at the silicon-controlled rectifier and try to get a better angle on the lens of Q_1. Also make certain the 9-V battery is operational.

The phototransistor used here is available from Radio Shack (#276-130). This particular device has exceptionally stable characteristics and high elimination sensitivity. It is used in low-power applications, as its maximum dissipation is only 200 mW. In the circuit shown here, the transistor need pass only a small amount of current required to trigger the SCR.

LOW-CURRENT AC RELAY

In recent years, optoelectronic devices have been used to perform a myriad of control and switching functions. One of the best known classes of optoelectronics involves a component that is known as an optoisolator. The optoisolator is contained in one package and allows one circuit to control another without any direct ac or dc connections. It does this by means of a light-emitting diode and a light-activated component such as a LASCR (light-activated silicon-controlled rectifier). Two LASCRs may be wired in reverse parallel to arrive at a light-activated triac. The General Electric H11J1 is an optoisolator that triggers a triac by means of the light from an internal LED. This device is shown schematically in Fig. 6-15.

When current is passed through the LED, it glows and causes the internal triac to conduct. Note that there is no direct connection between the LED circuit and that which is controlled by the triac.

Figure 6-16 shows how the GE H11J1 is used in a low-current ac relay circuit. The optoisolator is housed in a mini-DIP package containing six pins. It can be connected directly to a small section of perf board. A high-value gate resistance circuit is connected across the ac line, which is switched by the triac. A low-voltage source is connected to the LED input which will draw approximately 12 mA.

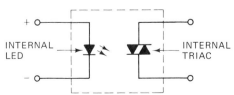

FIGURE 6-15 General Electric H11J1 optoisolator. (Courtesy General Electric.)

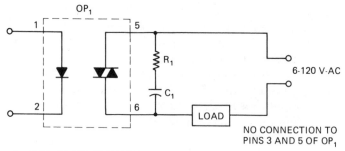

C$_1$: 0.02 μF DISK, 1000 V DC

OP$_1$: GE H11J1

R$_1$: 100-Ω, 1-W CARBON

FIGURE 6-16 Low-current ac relay circuit. (Courtesy General Electric.)

Often this is a 1.5-V battery with a series-connected switch. When the switch is thrown in the LED circuit, it triggers the triac, and power is connected to the load. The tiny optoisolator is capable of passing only about 50 mA of current, so only low-powered circuits can be directly controlled by this project. Voltage values to the load may range from 6 to 120 V ac. This means that power transformers may be turned on and off as well as small light bulbs and many other ac-only devices.

Figure 6-17 shows a suggested triggering circuit for the internal LED, although any low-voltage source capable of delivering 12 mA of current will work as well. Circuits such as these are often coupled to the logic outputs of computers to allow for computer control of ac loads.

Certainly the same basic switching function could be accomplished using a low-current relay or even a solid-state switch directly connected to the control circuit. This can prevent problems should a component breakdown occur. In such instances, it is possible for the control circuit to be placed across the ac line. This would immediately destroy many computer logic circuits. By using the optoisolator, it is nearly impossible for this to occur, as there is no direct connection between the two control sections.

If you do not wish to install the battery activator, you can prob-

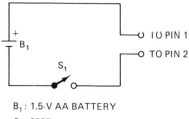

B$_1$: 1.5-V AA BATTERY

S$_1$: SPST

FIGURE 6-17 Activation circuit.

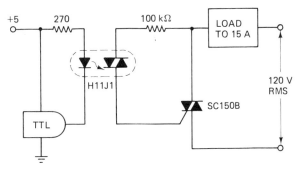

LOGIC ZERO SUPPLIES POWER TO LOAD

FIGURE 6-18 Optoisolator circuit used to trigger high-current triac. (Courtesy General Electric.)

ably build the entire circuit on a 1-in. square section of perf board. This allows you to incorporate this circuit inside an existing computer or other logic device, possibly including some of the "pocket computers" which are becoming quite popular.

TRANSISTOR-TRANSISTOR LOGIC (TTL) CONTROL CIRCUITS. The optoisolator, as previously mentioned, excels in logic circuits where a logic output must be used to trigger and control ac devices. Figures 6-18 through 6-20 are circuits designed by General Electric using the H11J1 as the interface between the TTL device and the power circuit. Figure 6-18 is a circuit used for resistive loads in noncritical applications. Here the internal triac controls an external triac, one which is rated to handle a current of 15 A (resistive) at 120 V ac. The next circuit is capable of handling 25 A at 120 V ac and is designed for inductive loads and critical applications. The latter circuit offers good noise immunity. The third circuit is designed

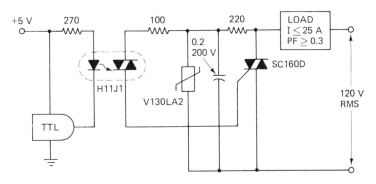

LOGIC ZERO SUPPLIES POWER TO LOAD

FIGURE 6-19 TTL-driven circuit. (Courtesy General Electric.)

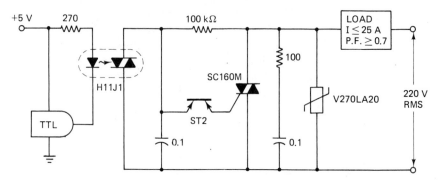

FIGURE 6-20 Another optoisolator circuit offering excellent noise and overvoltage capabilities. (Courtesy General Electric.)

to work at industrial voltages and offers excellent noise and overvoltage capabilities.

All these circuits use the low-current H11J1 optoisolator but tack on outboard components which allow for the handling of high amounts of current. These extra components will require very large heat sinks, owing to the high amounts of current which may be drawn. Note that in every case the load current is controlled by the switching of an external triac which incorporates the internal triac of the H11J1 in the gate circuits. The load circuit is completely isolated from the control circuit (the TTL device). This particular General Electric optoisolator offers complete isolation between the two circuit legs up to a dc potential of over 5000 V and an ac potential of about 4000 V rms.

DIODE CRYSTAL SWITCH

Many commercial and home-brew radio receivers and transmitters still depend on individual quartz crystals to control frequency. Crystal-controlled circuits have the advantage of being extremely stable as far as frequency output is concerned and rival even the best variable-frequency oscillators in this area. There are disadvantages, however—namely, the need for many crystals in order to tune many different frequencies. The output frequency of a crystal-controlled oscillator can be varied slightly, but to move up and down the band, most circuits are equipped with two or more crystal sockets and a switch which selects the crystal to be used in the circuit. Here is where a major problem can develop. When switch contacts close, a resistance is created (albeit slight). This is usually no problem at first, but as the switch ages and collects dust and other foreign matter, the resistance can increase or fluctuate with each activation. The added resistance will change the frequency at which the crystal oscillates by a small amount. However, the outputs from most crystal oscillators are usually multiplied, sometimes by 20 times or more. Any frequency change at the crystal will also be multiplied, making a mountain out of a molehill.

The circuit shown in Fig. 6-21 was added to a crystal-controlled transmitter I used for amateur radio operations. The original circuit contained four crystal sockets and a small variable capacitor between one pin of each and ground for tuning purposes. The schematic drawing shows the original circuit and below it the solid-state switching circuit that was added. The four diodes serve as the solid-state switches. They are controlled by a standard mechanical switch, which connects them to a 12-V dc internal supply through carbon resistors. Only the crystal above the diode which is switched into the circuit is activated. The 12-V supply is sampled, feeding current to the diode. It conducts and completes the crystal circuit to ground. No mechanical switching is used directly within the crystal circuit. Current is switched in a separate circuit leg, causing diode conducting and eliminating many of the problems discussed previously.

This circuit is designed for installation within the transmitter or receiver and gets its power from the internal 12-V source. Use a high-quality ceramic rotary switch for S_1. First, you will have to un-

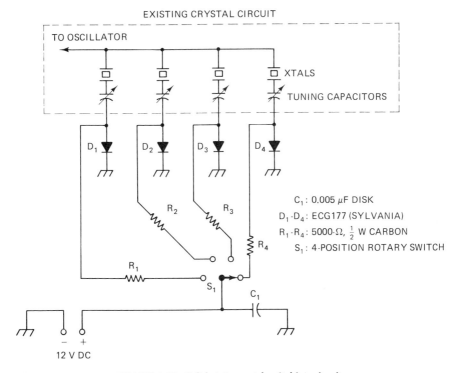

FIGURE 6-21 Solid-state crystal switching circuit.

ground the crystal circuit. This can best be done by clipping the switch lead at the bottom of each capacitor. At each unterminated capacitor, connect a resistor and diode, as indicated in the schematic drawing. Connect the opposite end of each diode to the previous ground points. Keep all leads as short as possible. Now mount the rotary switch close enough to the crystal socket to allow for connection of the remaining resistor leads. Again, keep these short. If you add too much extraneous wiring, you will add capacitance to the circuit. The rotary contact of S_1 is then attached to the existing 12-V dc supply and bypassed with a .005-μF disk-ceramic capacitor.

The switch which was originally installed to mechanically change crystals in my transmitter was not of good quality, so I used a new one. However, you can probably use the original switch to forward-bias the diodes in this circuit if it is of high-quality construction. This gets around many of the mechanical problems involved in the installation of a new switch.

To test the circuit, activate your transmitter or receiver as you normally would. You may find it necessary to touch up the crystal trimmers a bit, as circuit resistance may have changed. You should get stable frequency control from your crystal oscillator and switching frequencies (crystals) will be smooth and drift-free.

VOICE-ACTUATED SWITCH

A voice-actuated switch is a circuit which opens or closes switch contacts whenever someone speaks. With the availability of inexpensive silicon-controlled rectifiers and triacs, these devices are quite simple and can be built with a minimum of components at a low cost. Such circuits are often used to trigger tape recorders, radio transmitters, and other devices, although for transmitting purposes, special anticipatory subcircuits are included which are fast to activate and slow to turn off.

Figure 6-22 shows a basic voice-actuated circuit which uses a triac to control a 115-V ac relay. Input is obtained from an audio amplifier such as might be used in a PA system. Alternately, you can use the PA output from a citizens band transceiver. You can even connect the circuit to the speaker terminal of a stereo system and use music as the actuator. T_1 accepts the audio-frequency output from the amplifier at its primary winding. The secondary winding is used to supply cut-on current to the gate circuit of the triac. R_1 is used as a means of controlling the cut-on sensitivity. This circuit is designed for connection to the terminals of an 8-Ω speaker, but if your audio amplifier is set up for a different output impedance, choose a transformer which will reflect this. For example, some amplifiers

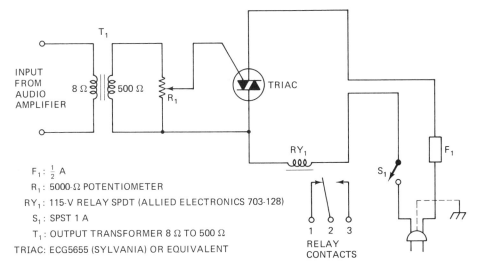

INPUT
FROM
AUDIO
AMPLIFIER

8 Ω   500 Ω R_1 TRIAC

T_1

RY_1 S_1 F_1

F_1: $\frac{1}{2}$ A

R_1: 5000-Ω POTENTIOMETER

RY_1: 115-V RELAY SPDT (ALLIED ELECTRONICS 703-128)

S_1: SPST 1 A

T_1: OUTPUT TRANSFORMER 8 Ω TO 500 Ω

TRIAC: ECG5655 (SYLVANIA) OR EQUIVALENT

1   2   3
RELAY
CONTACTS

FIGURE 6-22   Voice-actuated switching circuit.

have 600-Ω outputs. Here it would be most appropriate to use a one-to-one matching transformer with a 600-Ω primary and a 600-Ω secondary. Actually, the secondary impedance is noncritical, and many different values will work well.

The triac used in this circuit can safely pass up to 800 mA, so it is very overrated in driving the relay, which draws less than 50 mA. You may wish to substitute other relays, however, so the use of this triac will give you a lot of flexibility in making the choice. Power for the relay is obtained from the 115-V ac line. The line is fused for $\frac{1}{2}$ A, which is adequate to protect the relay and triac specified.

The circuit is installed on a 5-in. square section of perforated circuit board. This should provide adequate room for all the components, with the exception of R_1 and S_1, which will be mounted through the walls of the enclosure. I used a plastic case for my circuit, but one made from aluminum will serve as well. If you use a metal case, be sure to ground it to the ground pin of the line plug. The case is drilled to accept the shaft of R_1 and S_1. You will also want to install a two-terminal input strip for connection to the audio amplifier and another one to access the relay contacts. The fuse may be installed on the circuit board, in an appropriate holder mounted through the enclosure wall, or as an in-line device. I used a miniature output transformer which took up very little space and could be circuit-board-mounted, but if you have a larger model in your junk box, you can just as easily mount it to the circuit case. Insulated hookup wire is used to connect R_1 to the transformer secondary and to the gate circuit of the triac. Two more lengths are used to connect S_1 in series with one side of the 115-V line.

Operation of this circuit is quite simple. Connect the audio amplifier output to the transformer primary and provide a steady input to the microphone by whistling. Now adjust R_1 until you hear the relay contacts activate. It will be necessary to readjust R_1 each time the acoustic input to the microphone drops significantly. You are now free to use the relay contacts to switch outboard circuits. The relay specified will switch up to 10 A at 115 V ac or up to the same value at 30 V dc. The contacts are equivalent to a single-pole double-throw switch. When the relay is not activated, the movable contact engages a fixed one. When energized, the relay causes the movable contact to switch to the opposite fixed contact. This circuit can be used to switch power to other devices, to cut speakers and other components out of a circuit, and for a myriad of other purposes.

LIGHT-TRIGGERED SCR SWITCH

Silicon-controlled rectifiers present an open circuit until adequate current flows in the gate circuit, causing it to fire. This means that the diode conducts (like any other diode) and that current may flow to the load. When ac circuits are used to drive SCRs, the output is always direct current. Batteries and other dc power supplies may also be used as the driving source, with the SCR acting merely as a switch rather than a switch and a rectifier. Current flow within the gate circuit is usually controlled by a separate resistor (usually variable), which samples the main circuit current, creating a separate circuit leg between gate and anode.

The circuit shown in Fig. 6-23 was designed for low-current operation using a 9-V transistor radio battery as the power source. Its main function is to supply latching current to RY_1, a miniature relay. The gate circuit draws very little current, but many relays require a lot. The relay I used was purchased at a local Radio Shack outlet and draws approximately 10 mA at 9 V dc. Other relays may be used as well, but they must have the capability of operating from a 9-V source. If they draw much more than 10 to 15 mA, battery life will be shortened.

The only really unusual thing about this circuit is the method used to trigger the SCR. This is a light-activated circuit, and the relay will trigger when a light source is directed across the sensitized surface of PC_1, an inexpensive photocell, which was also purchased at Radio Shack. Technically, PC_1 is known as a cadmium-sulfide cell, but it may also be known as a light-activated resistor. The cadmium-sulfide cell is a passive device, requiring no current for operation.

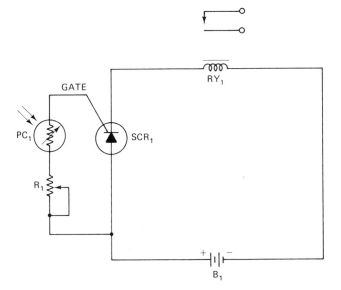

B₁ : 9-V BATTERY
C₁ : 50 μF 12 V DC
PC₁ : PHOTOCELL (RADIO SHACK 276-116)
R₁ : 5000-Ω, $\frac{1}{2}$ W POTENTIOMETER
RY₁ : LOW-CURRENT RELAY (RADIO SHACK)
SCR₁ : RCA   SK3950/5400

FIGURE 6-23   Light-triggered SCR switch.

It contains a small window on the top of its case which exposes the crystalline surface. In complete darkness, the cell presents a resistance of approximately 500,000 Ω, but when subjected to bright light, this value will decrease to about 100 Ω. You can vary the resistance by increasing and decreasing the brilliance of the light source.

With this in mind, it can be seen that the gate circuit of the SCR consists of two variable resistors. R_1 is the standard type, while PC_1 is varied by changing light intensities. These two devices in the gate circuit will allow you to control the miniature relay with a flashlight or other source of illumination.

I used an RCA SK3950 silicon-controlled rectifier for this circuit, although hundreds of other types will serve just as well. This device may be operated at up to 30 V and will pass a maximum current of 800 mA. This is about 10 times that required by the relay, but bear in mind that the small 9-V battery is very limited in output power. Any SCR which is capable of conducting current of the value needed to trigger the relay used with this circuit will suffice.

I elected to build most of the circuit on a 4-in. square section of perf board and installed the relay, SCR, and battery on its surface.

The entire assembly was then mounted in a small plastic enclosure that was drilled to accept R_1 and PC_1. The enclosure arrangement is shown in Fig. 6-24. The variable resistor was mounted in the upper left-hand corner of the front panel, while the relay terminal strip was installed at the lower right-hand corner. The top of the enclosure was used to mount PC_1. Two small holes were drilled through the plastic surface to accept the photocell's two leads, which were connected directly to the circuit board. Three-inch lengths of insulated hookup wire were used to connect R_1. Using epoxy cement, a $1\frac{1}{2}$-in. cardboard tube was mounted over PC_1. This serves to keep ambient light from triggering the circuit and may be modified to suit individual needs. The longer the tube, the more protection provided. When this circuit is not to be operated, a small wad of paper shoved in the tube opening will serve as an off switch. Alternately, a miniature toggle switch may be mounted on the front panel in series with one of the battery leads.

To test the circuit, connect an ohmmeter across the relay output terminals. Now direct the beam from a flashlight onto the photocell and adjust R_1 until the relay contacts engage. At this point, the meter will read 0 Ω. This assumes that you have installed a relay with normally open contacts. If yours has normally closed contacts, the meter will read 0 Ω before circuit activation and infinite resistance when the relay engages. After the relay is activated, back off on R_1 a bit and remove the light source. The relay should now disengage. If not, back off on R_1 a bit more. Keep making these adjustments until you can engage the relay with the light source alone.

Since this circuit will be used for a multitude of purposes and with many different light sources, it is possible to run into activation or deactivation problems using the gate circuit in the schematic draw-ing. If you have trouble getting the relay to activate with your light source, try connecting a 5-kΩ potentiometer in parallel with the photo-cell. This will lower its internal resistance considerably (depending

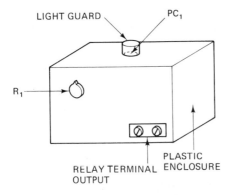

LIGHT GUARD   PC$_1$

R$_1$

RELAY TERMINAL
OUTPUT

PLASTIC
ENCLOSURE

FIGURE 6-24   Enclosure preparation.

on its setting) and will make activation at lower light levels much easier. In most instances, however, this will not be necessary. If the relay is being continually triggered by ambient light sources, increasing the resistance of R_1 should solve the problem.

Using this circuit, you can control ac and dc power to many different types of devices by connecting the relay contacts in series with their power sources. Make sure any device connected here does not draw more current than the relay contacts can handle. A miniature relay has been used here, and its contact ratings may not be high enough to control all devices. You can, however, increase the power-handling capability by using the small relay to switch current to the coil of a larger relay, one with higher current ratings. When the miniature relay engages, the larger one will do the same, and the latter component will then be used for external device switching.

SCR LIGHTNING SENSOR

A silicon-controlled rectifier does not conduct until an adequate trigger current flows in the gate circuit. Connecting a suitable resistor between the device anode and gate will cause current to flow. The diode then becomes forward biased and conducts current just like any other diode. Silicon-controlled rectifiers are often used as solid-state switches to turn current flow on and off. They may also be used as voltage control devices by adjusting the amount of conduction within the gate circuit.

The circuit shown in Fig. 6-25 uses the SCR as a switch. A standard gate circuit consisting of a variable resistor is used, but an additional circuit component is also incorporated which allows the solid-state switch to be controlled by lightning flashes. This additional component is merely a length of conductor (20 ft or more) which can be extended through a window, to the roof of a home or building, or even within the rooms of a home. During a thunderstorm, lightning flashes send out bursts of power which can be detected in much the same fashion as radio broadcasts. The pickup wire in this circuit is designed to pick up or detect some of this electricity and cause the SCR to fire. When this happens, a relay between the anode and cathode of the SCR is activated. Such circuits are often used to shut down electrical equipment during thunderstorms or even to ground external antennas in order to avoid a direct damaging hit. Citizens band and amateur radio operators have been using circuits such as these for quite a few years. In antenna applications, the relay is connected between the active elements and ground (usually at the end of the transmission line). When the circuit fires, the relay engages and shorts the entire structure to earth ground.

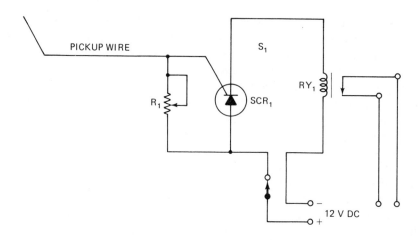

R₁ : 5 kΩ LINEAR TAPER (ALLIED ELECTRONICS 854-7314)
RY₁ : 12-V LATCHING RELAY
S₁ : SPST
SCR₁ : 50 PIV, 1 A (RCA SK3638)

FIGURE 6-25   SCR lightning sensor.

The relay used is a latching type. Since a lightning flash is of very short duration, a standard nonlatching relay would be activated for an instant or so and then switched to the off state as soon as the pulsed current terminated. The latching relay, however, needs only a short burst of current to move to the active state. It remains in this mode until manually disengaged.

The SCR you choose for this circuit should be a small-current type. High-current types will work but will require higher triggering currents. The forward current of the device need only be adequate to handle the current demand of the relay (and then for only a split second). You can probably mount everything on a small piece of perf board, including the relay. Alternately, you can use a terminal strip to install all components. The variable resistor sets device sensitivity. This will allow you to control just how close a storm has to be in order to bring about relay engagement. For maximum sensitivity, R_1 is adjusted to the point where conduction occurs and is then backed off slightly. You want the SCR to be right on the verge of firing. The added current needed to push the diode into conduction will be provided by static electricity brought on by the lightning flash.

Unless you have a device to generate static electricity, you will have to wait for a thunderstorm to test operation. Make certain that you can trigger the relay with R_1, back off on this component, and then begin stringing your pickup wire. The highest sensitivity will be accomplished by using the longest wire possible. Then when a thunderstorm develops in your area, note the action of this circuit. Back off on R_1 further to decrease the sensitivity.

In practical applications, this circuit is usually set and then forgotten. It will be checked after each storm in order to set the relay. Battery current is almost nonexistent, and shelf life can be expected. You can use this circuit with a 9-V transistor radio battery as long as the relay is designed for operation at this potential. The SPST switch is used to completely deactivate the circuit and removes all power when its contacts are opened.

You can connect any type of circuit to the relay switch contacts, but make certain that current flow does not exceed the contact rating. You may wish to install a larger relay at RY_1's terminals, controlling the former's power supply through the series connection. A larger relay is more appropriate for direct grounding of antennas which sometimes will take a lightning hit.

This circuit uses a dc latching relay, since the output from the SCR will always be direct current. If you wish to build the same circuit using an ac relay, a triac will be required. This circuit is shown in Fig. 6-26. It is necessary to change the value of the variable resistor due to the higher input voltage, but other than this and the triac substitution, the circuit is about the same as the previous one and accomplishes exactly the same thing.

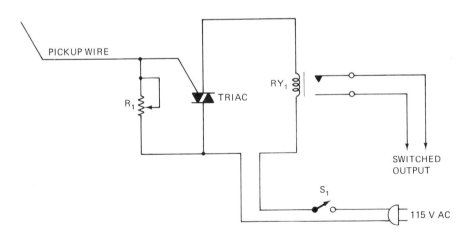

R$_1$: 25,000 Ω, 1 W (ALLIED ELECTRONICS 854-7329)

RY$_1$: 120-V AC LATCHING RELAY (ANY TYPE DRAWING LESS THAN 250 MA)

TRIAC: 200 PRV, LOW-CURRENT TYPE (RCA   SK3583)

S$_1$: SPST

FIGURE 6-26 Triac lightning detector.

DIODE SCRAMBLER

A balanced modulator is an electronic circuit which mixes an audio input with a carrier signal to produce a double-sideband audio output at the carrier frequency. The carrier itself is greatly suppressed. This is the first stage in a single-sideband transmitter. Later, one sideband is filtered out, and all the transmit power is wrapped up in a single sideband.

Figure 6-27 shows a basic balanced modulator circuit which consists of four germanium diodes connected in what would be known as a full-wave bridge configuration if used for power supply applications. Here, however, the input is carried through completely to the output, and the diode modulator is used to mix the carrier input with the audio. The resulting output will be two combined frequencies which are equal to the sum of the audio frequency and the carrier frequency and the difference between these two frequencies.

This same circuit may be used for scrambling audio signals. For these purposes, the carrier input is usually held to within 5 kHz, and the audio input is obtained from a small preamplifier. A double-sideband output sounds something like the human speech pattern when the nose is squeezed. There is a nasal whining which often sounds like the Donald Duck cartoon character, except not as intelligible. Oh, you may be able to identify a word or so, but even this is unlikely.

The idea here is to connect the double-sideband output (which is still at audio frequencies) to the input of a telephone line in order

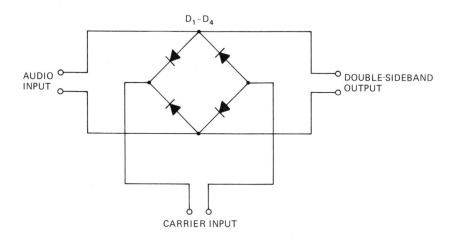

D_1-D_4: ECG109 (SYLVANIA)

FIGURE 6-27 **Diode scrambler.**

to transmit scrambled audio. At the receiving end, an identical circuit is attached to the output of the phone line, and a carrier input of the same frequency used at the scrambler is provided. The circuit will now act like a detector, and demodulated output will be the result.

This entire circuit may be constructed on a 1-in. square section of perf board. It will be necessary to test the forward resistance of each of the ECG109 diodes in order to arrive at four which are nearly identical. There are some slight internal differences which may be found from component to component, so those which are noticeably different from the others should be omitted and replaced with components which are more closely matched. The finished circuit may be installed in a small plastic enclosure, which can be connected directly to the phone line terminals. A pair of two-terminal connectors should be mounted to the enclosure, one to accept the output from the audio preamplifier and the other to accept the carrier input which may be provided by an audio-frequency generator. An identical circuit may be made up for connection to the receiving end of the telephone line.

To operate the circuit, simply set the audio generator to 4 kHz or so and have the party at the other end of the phone line do the same. You may now speak into the microphone for a scrambled telephone conversation. In most instances, it will be necessary to connect a small matching transformer whose primary winding is the same as the impedance of the preamplifier output. The secondary winding should be rated at 600 Ω. For demodulation purposes, the output should be connected to a transformer with a 600-Ω primary and a secondary winding rated to match the impedance of the audio amplifier input.

When using audio-frequency carriers, diode matching is not all that important. But always use identical components from the same manufacturer. This circuit may also be used to build single-sideband transmitters. Here diode matching is very important for the best audio quality.

ZENER KNEE TEST CIRCUIT

Zener diodes are solid-state devices which conduct only when a specific dc potential is reached. This breakover voltage point is often called the zener knee. A 12-V zener diode has a zener knee of 12 V dc. When this value is exceeded, the device conducts heavily. When used in conjunction with a series-connected resistor, zener diodes are valuable voltage regulators.

No two zener diodes are exactly alike. Two identical components from the same manufacturer and with the same zener knee rating will actually be slightly different. Therefore, if you should connect two identical zener diodes in parallel across a power supply output, the one with the lowest breakover point will conduct first. The difference is often measured in fractions of a volt, but in critical applications it is sometimes necessary to take note of the differences in components with equal ratings.

The circuit shown in Fig. 6-28 is a zener diode tester which allows you to compare the breakover voltage rating of a test component with another zener used as a reference. The circuit is a dc power supply which can be constructed in the same manner described for many others in this book. The difference is found at the output, where sockets are installed. In my tester, I used miniature crystal sockets, but any type which will allow for the insertion of the zener leads will suffice. The first socket is installed across the dc output lines and will contain the reference diode. The second socket is connected in a similar manner, except that there is a break between its bottom connector and the negative output. At this point in the circuit, a third socket is installed. This will be the metering point.

You may mount the sockets on top of the power supply enclosure and use insulated hookup wire to access the various circuit points. Make certain that you have free access to all three, because it will be necessary to insert diodes and test probes during every test.

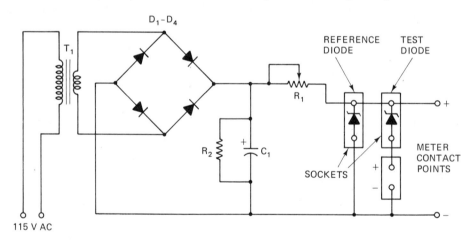

C$_1$: 100 µF, 50 V DC
D$_1$-D$_4$: 50 PIV, 1 A
R$_1$: 500-Ω, 10-W RHEOSTAT
R$_2$: 10 kΩ, $\frac{1}{2}$ W
T$_1$: 115 V PRIMARY, 12 V SECONDARY (SOUMA)

FIGURE 6-28 Zener diode test circuit.

When you complete the circuit (and before inserting any zener diodes), connect a dc voltmeter across the output and activate the supply. You should obtain a reading of approximately 17 V dc. Now insert a reference diode in the first socket. Adjust R_1 to the midway position and activate the supply again. The output voltage reading should be identical to the zener knee rating of the reference diode. For this discussion, let's assume that this value is 12 V dc. With the voltmeter still connected, increase the resistance of R_1 until the voltage begins to drop. This may not occur, but if it does, back off on R_1 slightly until the 12-V reading is again obtained. If you notice no drop-off, simply operate with R_1 in the maximum resistance position. Now insert the test diode after switching off the power supply. Remove the meter from the output leads and connect a milliammeter at the third socket. (Note the polarity markings.) Reactivate the power supply and note your meter reading. If you get no reading at all, the reference diode has a lower zener knee than the test diode. If the presence of current is indicated, then the test diode has a lower zener knee than the one in the reference position. Using a highly accurate dc voltmeter, you may even be able to note the differences in the output provided by various components.

This circuit was designed to do more than test zener diodes. It can also be used as a regulated power supply whose output may be changed by altering the value of a zener diode inserted in the reference socket alone. R_1 is adjusted to the maximum resistance which will still allow full zener output voltage when connected to a load.

NO-POWER CRYSTAL RECEIVER

Perhaps as a child you had the opportunity to receive a then-novel electronic device known as a crystal receiver. This was a small electronic circuit which would allow you to pick up your local radio station (listening through a miniature earphone) using no batteries or other on-board source of power. The crystal referred to in the name was really a type of diode. This component was used to rectify the miniscule amount of RF power which was picked up on the antenna. The pulsating dc current flow was then passed directly through the earphone, where it created an audio output. The previous project was really a crystal detector whose rectified output was fed to a micro-ammeter instead of an earphone.

The circuit shown in Fig. 6-29 is an AM radio which requires no on-board power. Its true operating power is the energy contained in the transmission of the broadcast station. High-frequency transmitting involves sending electrical energy out into space, and the crystal detector (and for that matter, all receiving devices) steals a

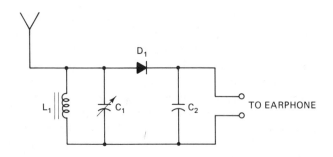

C$_1$: 365 pF VARIABLE (ALLIED ELECTRONICS 695-1000)

C$_2$: 0.005 μF DISK CERAMIC

D$_1$: ECG109 (SYLVANIA)

L$_1$: FERRITE ROD LOOPSTICK ANTENNA

FIGURE 6-29   Solid-state diode radio.

bit of this energy from the airwaves. It is then processed (rectified) and passed to a transducer (in this case, a crystal earphone).

While it is possible to obtain reception using a single diode alone and omitting the two capacitors and the inductor, such a circuit would be useful only in very close proximity to the radio station. For practical use, it is necessary to tune the RF energy. This allows a larger amount of power to be fed to the diode and thus to the earphone. Components L_1 and C_1 accomplish this. The remaining capacitor simply bypasses any RF energy to ground.

You can probably purchase the ferrite rod antenna at a local hobby store, or you may salvage one from a defunct transistor radio. Ferrite rod antennas consist of a large number of turns wound around a circular section of ferrous iron. The ferrite core magnifies the inductance and allows a high-value inductor to be of compact size. You can wind your own coil in an air-wound form, but it will be many times the size of the loopstick antenna. You can also purchase C_1 from your hobby store or salvage it from an old radio. This is wired in parallel with L_1 and allows you to tune the entire AM radio spectrum. The two components work together to make the circuit most sensitive to a station transmitting on a particular frequency and desensitize the circuit to other frequencies.

You can build this entire circuit on a small section of perf board. The actual size will depend on the size of the ferrite antenna. Some are only a few inches long, while others may be about 5 or more in. The tuning capacitor can be attached directly to the circuit board with epoxy cement. There are no polarity-conscious components here, and while D_1 is shown with its anode connected to C_1, a reversal here will make no difference whatsoever.

The crystal radio is dependent on the length of its antenna to a very high degree. You may get away with a very short antenna if you live close to a radio station. You may even be able to omit an external antenna altogether. In most applications, however, you will need at least a 3-ft length of small conductor wire which is hooked to the top of L_1/C_1. The longer the antenna, the more sensitive your receiver will be and the higher the output volume. In some outlying areas, far from any local radio stations, your antenna may have to be 20 or 30 ft long for adequate reception.

To operate the circuit, connect the high-impedance earphone at the output terminal and insert the device in your ear. You should hear a low-level hiss. Now, carefully tune C_1 until a station is heard. Don't expect overpowering volume, as you won't get it with this device. You will have to listen very carefully, but you should eventually hear a nearby broadcast station. If not, it will be necessary to reposition your antenna or to substantially increase its length. If you have a local radio station in your hometown, you should be able to hear it quite clearly and can listen day in and day out without any fear of discharging a nonexistent power source. There is no on-off switch on this device because it operates whenever the tuned radio station is on the air. It will operate 24 h a day, year after year.

This circuit is extremely simple, and hundreds upon hundreds of project books include variations of it in their pages. However, to make the project a little more interesting, a few modifications can be made to convert this AM radio into a self-powered FM radio which will tune the entire commercial FM band. It even goes one step further by allowing you to listen in on nearby aircraft broadcasts as well as the amateur radio 2-m band. You may even hear business band transmissions (fire, rescue, police, etc.).

The only modification required is at L_1 and C_1. The components specified in the original schematic must be removed and replaced with an LC circuit more appropriate for these VHF broadcasts. The inductor can be wound at home in a few minutes and consists of $4\frac{1}{2}$ turns of No. 16 wire, $\frac{3}{4}$ in. in diameter. Use tinned copper wire (insulated or not) to wind this coil, and space the turns evenly over a length of $\frac{1}{2}$ in. The variable capacitor should be a 0–15-pF trimmer. When these two components are inserted as replacements, the circuit will be most sensitive to broadcasts on frequencies of from 88 to 150 mHz. Often stations which operate at these frequencies produce lower-power outputs than some commercial AM stations, so the success of this circuit will depend on how close you are to these VHF broadcasters. You can use the same antenna as before, but you may also connect a television antenna, FM receiver antenna, or the like for improved results. Wiring is more critical if you opt for this modification. Keep the connections between L_1, C_1, and D_1 as short as possible. You will probably have to tune C_1 with a small screwdriver. This should be made entirely of plastic, as metallic types will add capacitance (and possibly inductance) while they are in contact with the tuning screw.

You may find that your circuit will not tune up to 150 mHz. If this is the case, pull the turns of the coil apart by a small amount. If your receiver is tuning too low, compress the turns a bit. With a little experimentation, you should be able to tune the full range of VHF broadcasts.

MINIATURE AMPLIFIER FOR CRYSTAL RECEIVERS

A crystal receiver is a useful device in emergency conditions when it is necessary to detect radio broadcasts without the aid of an on-board power source. In locations with a nearby radio station, the receiver may even take the place of a standard broadcast type owing to the increased volume. However, most of the time the crystal receiver is little more than a toy. The fact of the matter is that the volume level is usually so low that listening is difficult. Fortunately, you can have all the emergency advantages of a crystal receiver with a little more volume by using the battery-powered amplifier circuit shown in Fig. 6-30. This uses a single NPN transistor. An RCA type is specified here, but hundreds of others will work as well. The single transistor is powered by a penlite battery and boosts the low-level audio from the diode detector to a level which is more suitable for comfortable listening. No, the circuit won't break your eardrums. The output is still relatively low, but it's far superior to direct listening

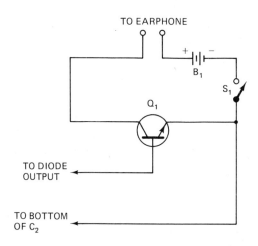

B$_1$: 1.5-V AA CELL

Q$_1$: SK3835

S$_1$: SPST (MINIATURE)

FIGURE 6-30 Transistor amplifier circuit for crystal radios.

on the crystal set. If you want, you may combine this circuit with the previous project, as very little additional circuit board space will be required. The transistor leads are pushed through the holes in the perf board. The negative battery terminal is connected to the transistor emitter, while the positive terminal attaches directly to the earphone lead. The remaining earphone connection is made directly to the transistor's collector electrode. The output from the diode is again direct connected, this time to the transistor base. The bottom of C_2 in the former circuit connects to the emitter. A miniature switch (S_1) can be included in this circuit. This will allow you to conserve battery life when the amplifier is not in use. To keep the circuit as small as possible and to avoid the problems associated with installing a switch on a piece of perforated circuit board, you may elect to omit the switch altogether and simply remove the battery from its holder after every use.

For the circuit to work properly, you must install the detector diode exactly as shown in the previous project. Without the amplifier, the polarity of the diode was unimportant, but here it is crucial. Of course, if you've already wired your crystal radio set with the diode reverse connected from that in the schematic drawing, you can simply substitute a PNP transistor for Q_1, such as the ECG3722.

To test the circuit, make the appropriate connections to your crystal radio and then activate S_1 while listening in the earphone. You should note a sizable increase in audio output, and your receiver is tuned as usual. Increasing the length of the receive antenna will still increase earphone volume, but with this additional audio amplifier circuit your listening volume will not be so critical. If you want to revert to a straight crystal radio again, simply break one of the connections to the amplifier and input the earphone at its former location.

SELF-DRIVEN FIELD STRENGTH METER

A field strength meter is a device which provides relative readings of the output from radio-frequency transmitters. The circuit is actually a simple detector very similar to that of a crystal radio. A short antenna samples a portion of the radiated wave when placed in fairly close proximity to the transmitting antenna. The radio-frequency energy is rectified and then passed on to a meter. Most such devices have a variable control which will allow the meter indicator to be adjusted to the midscale position. This is called the reference transmitter output, or reference reading. The transmitter will then be retuned or another transmitter used while leaving the field strength meter in the same position. If the meter indicates a higher than midscale reading, this is a sign of a power increase. A power decrease (when compared to reference) is evidenced by the indicator dropping below the midscale position.

Like a crystal radio, a basic field strength meter is powered from the radio-frequency signal itself, and as such, it requires no batteries or other source of operating current. This allows the device to be highly portable, and many are made so small that they will fit in a shirt pocket.

The circuit for a basic field strength meter is shown in Fig. 6-31. It consists of an inductor, diode rectifier, bypass capacitor, variable resistor, and miniature meter. None of the components are especially critical, and you can probably build the entire circuit from junk box components. You can even do away with the inductor if you plan to measure transmitter outputs of 500 W or more. Here you would simply connect the portion of the circuit which lies at the bottom of L_1 to a ground stake. However, the coil provides a bit of tuning of the RF energy for this circuit and makes it a lot more sensitive.

You can construct this circuit on a 2-in. square section of perforated circuit board, but even this is not necessary, as the meter terminals themselves serve as good connection points for most of the components. You would also want to install a five-contact terminal strip inside the metal or plastic enclosure (metal preferred) in order to mount L_1 and one end of D_1. The variable resistor is mounted through the front panel of the enclosure and is wired in series with

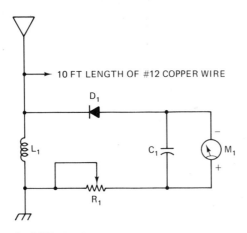

C$_1$: 0.005 μF DISK CERAMIC
D$_1$: ECG109 (SYLVANIA)
L$_1$: 2.4 MH RF CHOKE (ALLIED ELECTRONICS 855-3588)
M$_1$: 0.05 MICROAMMETER (ALLIED ELECTRONICS 270-1751)
R$_1$: 50-kΩ, 1-W POTENTIOMETER

FIGURE 6-31 Simple field strength meter.

the bottom of L_1 and the positive contact of M_1. Short lengths of insulated hookup wiring are used for this connection.

Some persons will choose to purchase a telescoping whip antenna for this circuit, but you can get away with using a 10-in. length of solid copper conductor, No. 12 or larger. You're not confined to the 10-in. length. As a matter of fact, longer antennas will pick up more RF energy and make the entire circuit more sensitive. This may be necessary if you wish to obtain readings from low-powered transmitter circuits such as CB transceivers.

When preparing the enclosure, be sure to ground the bottom of L_1 to the metal case. If a plastic case is used, provide a simple output terminal at this point for connection to an earth ground, if necessary. D_1 is a germanium diode, and almost any type will work in this circuit, although the one specified will probably provide the best sensitivity. You may find it necessary to change the value of R_1 in order to obtain the best linear adjustment of M_1. Transmitter output power will partially determine the ohmic value of R_1. If you find the variable resistor you have chosen to be a bit "touchy" as far as setting the needle indicator is concerned (needle seems to be full off and full on over a very slight rotation of R_1), decrease its ohmic value by half and try again. If you seem to get no control whatsoever of the meter and the needle is constantly pegged, double the value of R_1.

I chose a 0-50 microammeter for M_1 because it is the most sensitive meter (reads the lowest current values) of any widely available type and is quite commonly found at electronic hobby stores. However, if you have a microammeter, say, with a 0-500 range, you can probably get away with using it, although the sensitivity factor will be decreased by 10 times and more RF energy will be required to obtain a full-scale reading. The latter meter is most applicable to moderate- and high-power field strength measurements.

To test your circuit, simply extend the antenna and place it a few feet away from the transmit antenna. With R_1 in the maximum resistance position (fully counterclockwise) key the transmitter. If the meter goes full scale, then your resistor is not large enough and must be replaced with one of a higher ohmic value. Chances are, however, you will get little or no reading at all. With the transmitter still keyed, rotate R_1 until a midscale reading is obtained (25 μA). This will be your reference point. You can now attempt to retune the transmitter while observing the field strength reading. If the meter goes past midscale, this is an indication that your efforts have produced a higher-power output.

The field strength method of tuning any radio transmitter and/or antenna system is far better than cutting the antenna for minimum SWR. Especially in mobile applications, minimum SWR does not always produce the highest output power. In my mobile setup, I have found that my short, coil-loaded antenna radiates the most RF energy when the SWR reads just over 2 to 1. This will vary from installation to installation. When the field strength meter reads the highest, this is when maximum output power is obtained. Most field strength measurements should be made at least 6 ft from the antenna. In moderate- to high-powered installations, you may be able to get 100 ft or more away, which provides an even better indication.

SUPER-SENSITIZING YOUR FIELD STRENGTH METER. For micropower applications, the field strength meter shown will probably leave a lot to be desired. You can, however, increase the sensitivity several thousand times by adding the circuit shown in Fig. 6-32. As you can see, this is far more complex than the original field strength meter but will provide you with the capability of obtaining field strength measurements when transmit output power is in the milliwatt range. The circuit is a meter amplifier and will accept the output from the original field strength meter and boost it many times

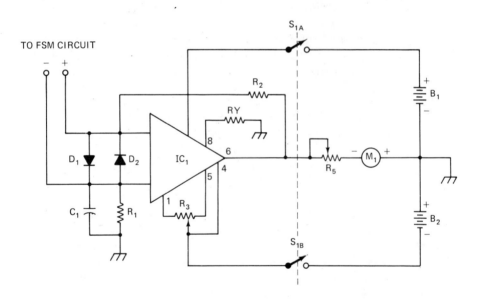

B_1-B_2: 1.5 V AA CELLS

C_1: 0.1 μF CAPACITOR

D_1-D_2: 1N914

IC$_1$: LM4250 (NATIONAL SEMICONDUCTOR)

M$_1$: 0-50 MICROAMPERES

R_1-R_2: 1.5 MΩ

R_3: 100-Ω, $\frac{1}{2}$ W CONTROL (LINEAR TAPER)

R_4: 10 MΩ

R_5: 10-Ω, $\frac{1}{2}$ W CONTROL (LINEAR TAPER)

S_1: DPST MINIATURE

NOTE: ALL FIRED RESISTORS ARE $\frac{1}{2}$ W CARBON

FIGURE 6-32 Amplifier for field strength meter.

to the meter contained at the output of IC pin 6. This circuit should be constructed on a 4-in. square section of perforated circuit board. The field strength meter circuit may be wired directly to the input of the IC, and the combined circuits can then be installed in a single enclosure. This amplifier requires two penlite batteries, which are connected as shown to supply positive and negative operating power to the IC. Keep all component leads as short as possible. Again, a 0-50 microammeter has been chosen, but other microammeters may be used as well. To connect this amplifier to the field strength meter, simply remove the original meter and connect the IC input leads to the former positive and negative meter contacts.

To operate this circuit, key a low-powered transmitter, activate S_1, and adjust R_3 and R_5 for a midscale meter reading. Do not use this circuit around high-powered transmitters, as the drive will be far too high. You will also find it necessary to adjust the variable resistor in the original field strength meter circuit to provide the needed input to the IC. Once this has been set, it may be left in place, or a fixed resistor may be substituted.

HIGH-POWERED RELATIVE OUTPUT METER

Several decades ago, the tuning of RF transmitters and amplifiers was accomplished by "peaking the grids and dipping the plates." This meant that grid current to the final amplifier tube or tubes was set to maximum, while plate current was set to minimum. This was done by observing two meters, one to measure grid current and the other plate current while adjusting the appropriate controls. Today, however, most single-sideband transmitters and linear amplifiers are tuned for maximum output power. Theoretically, this will occur when the grids are peaked and the plates are dipped, but in actual practice this is not always the case. Often the amplifier will operate slightly out of plate dip and provide maximum output power with minimum distortion. For home-brewed transmitters and amplifiers, maximum output tuning may be accomplished by using an outboard relative power meter, which may be connected directly to the antenna output terminal. Alternately, a field strength meter may be used which picks up a sampling of the transmitter output and uses no direct connections.

The circuit shown in Fig. 6-33 is designed to be incorporated in a high-powered transmitter or linear amplifier, but it may also be installed in a separate enclosure and attached to the transmitter output with a T connector, one side of which goes directly to the antenna. I used this circuit in a home-brew linear amplifier which produced a peak output of about 1400 W. It provides a relative indication of

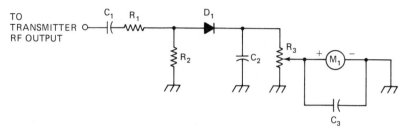

C₁ : 0.001 7000-V "DOOR KNOB" CAPACITOR

C₂-C₃ : 0.01 µF 1000 V DC DISK CERAMIC

D₁ : SK3087 (RCA)

M₁ : DC MA (0–1 MA) (ALLIED ELECTRONICS   910-4560)

R₁ : 10 Ω, 2 W CARBON

R₂ : 1000 Ω, 2 W CARBON

R₃ : 25 Ω, 2-W POTENTIOMETER (ALLIED ELECTRONICS   753-5067)

FIGURE 6-33 **High-powered RF voltage detector.**

RF power output and will allow you to tune the final amplifier to maximum levels.

The circuit is built on perf board and uses a 0–1 milliammeter as the power indicator. Microammeters may also be used, but it will be necessary to increase the value of R_3 by 5 to 10 times. A doorknob capacitor (C_1) is used to sample the RF output. This is a 7000-V unit and is quite a bit oversized for this circuit, since only a small amount of RF current will be drawn. For most applications, a disk-ceramic capacitor rated at 1000 V or more should do well. It will also be a bit easier to mount to the circuit board due to its smaller size.

Wiring is not especially critical. Just make certain there are no wiring errors, as this could bring about extremely heavy loading at the transmitter output. All components, with the exception of R_3 and M_1 (and its bypass capacitor, C_3), are mounted on the perf board. Tie all the ground leads together and short them to the transmitter or amplifier chassis.

R_3 and M_1 are mounted through the enclosure case, while C_3 is connected directly across the meter terminals. The detector diode (D_1) must be connected as shown, or the meter will read in reverse. Hookup wiring is used to connect M_1 to R_3 and R_3 to the output of D_1. The remaining terminals of R_3 and M_1 are connected to the chassis ground. Past the point where D_1 enters the circuit, dc current is flowing, so the hookup wiring leads do not need to be terribly short. However, if they are unnecessarily long, RF energy may be picked up from the amplifier tank coil, creating havoc with your meter readings. If your design requires sizable lengths of hookup wire, install a .01-µF disk-ceramic capacitor between these leads and ground to short out any RF current which may flow.

The circuit is completed by connecting the input directly to the RF output terminal of the transmitter or amplifier. This is best accomplished by making a solder connection directly to the antenna terminal. Testing is quite simple and starts by rotating R_3 to its maximum resistance position. This means that the positive terminal of M_1 is effectively shorted to ground. Now activate your transmitter-amplifier and tune up in a normal manner. Slowly rotate R_3 until you obtain a half-scale reading on M_1. Now readjust the drive, plate, and output controls until a maximum reading is obtained at M_1. Tuning up in the normal manner will yield a near-maximum output, but tweaking the controls while observing M_1 should get you a small percentage increase. When maximum output power is obtained, you can be sure your amplifier is operating at peak efficiency and with minimum distortion characteristics. You can then decrease power output by backing off on the drive if desired.

This circuit does not read power output directly; that is, it does not give you a reading in watts. You can, however, calibrate your meter (while operating into a dummy antenna) with an accurate wattmeter. For instance, with R_1 in a set position, an output of 1000 W (as measured by the wattmeter) may result in a meter indication of .8 mA. In the future, anytime M_1 gives this same reading, you will know that you are putting out approximately 1000 W. Of course, when you operate your amplifier into different loads, the power will change accordingly. This meter calibration is good only when operating into impedances which are identical to that of the dummy load. For this reason, this circuit is far more valuable as a tuning aid than as an accurate power output indicator. *Caution:* This circuit is by no means a dummy load. It does not take the place of any antenna, so your amplifier must always be terminated in an appropriate load to prevent damage to its tubes or transistors.

DUMMY ANTENNA RF VOLTMETER

Many electronic experimenters have built nonradiating antennas which are better known as *dummy loads*. This is a circuit into which a radio transmitter may be operated for testing purposes and radiates little or no RF energy. Dummy loads are simply noninductive resistors, usually measuring 50 Ω, which absorb all the transmitter power. Dummy loads are indispensable for transmitter checkout under normal operating conditions, but most are not equipped to tell you what your output power is.

The circuit shown in Fig. 6-34 will not indicate the exact level of power output, but when used with a multimeter, it can offer you relative output indications. This circuit samples a small amount of

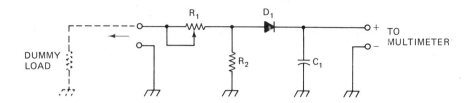

C$_1$: 0.01 μF DISK CERAMIC
D$_1$: ECG109 (SYLVANIA)
R$_1$: 150 Ω, 1 W VARIABLE
R$_2$: 1200 Ω, $\frac{1}{2}$ W CARBON

FIGURE 6-34   RF meter to be used with a dummy antenna and multimeter.

the RF voltage at the dummy load, rectifies it, and provides an output voltage which can be measured on a multimeter set to read dc voltage. Again, this circuit is used for relative power measurement. Variable resistor R_1 allows control of the amount of sampled voltage passed on to the rectifier in order to use your multimeter at a voltage scale which will provide better than half-scale indicator deflection. Relative measurements are taken by inputting power to the dummy load of a known value. The multimeter is adjusted by means of R_1 to give a, say, $\frac{3}{4}$-scale reading. Different transmitters may now be used to input the dummy load, or the power from the original transmitter may be increased or decreased. R_1 is left untouched for these subsequent readings, and the meter is watched to see if power has increased or decreased. If the indicator drops to half-scale, this is an indication that power has been cut by about one-third. If it rises to full scale, this indicates a 25% increase in transmitter power.

The entire circuit is built on a small piece of perforated circuit board and mounted in an aluminum enclosure. This is necessary to keep the RF energy confined in order to prevent radiation. Figure 6-35 shows the circuit board layout. Note that the variable resistor is left off the circuit board. This will be mounted through the aluminum case. The inset shows how the 150-kΩ potentiometer is to be wired. If you should accidentally reverse the connection of D_1 into this circuit, this is really no problem. The positive and negative output terminals will simply be reversed.

I was able to obtain a miniature aluminum enclosure measuring 3 in. wide, 2 in. high, and 4 in. long. One side was drilled to accept the shaft of R_1, and 1-in. bolts with $\frac{3}{4}$-in. spacers were used to mount the circuit board. Matching nuts keep the board firmly in place. My dummy load was very much like the Heathkit commercial model which uses a 50-Ω noninductive resistor immersed in a gallon can of oil. I mounted my circuit and its enclosure on top of the can and ac-

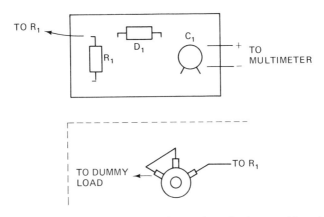

FIGURE 6-35 Component layout for previous circuit on perf board.

cessed the internal resistor by a small hole drilled through the lid. You may not be able to use this type of arrangement, but make certain the accessed lead to the resistor is shielded. This same circuit may be used some distance away from the dummy load by fitting the enclosure with an appropriate connector and using coaxial cable between it and dummy load.

To test your circuit, make certain R_1 is at its maximum resistance position. Connect a dc voltmeter to the output terminals and set the scale to the highest voltage possible. Now, apply RF power to the dummy load and then rotate the shaft of R_1 about halfway. Step your multimeter down to the lower ranges until your meter begins to provide an indication. When the needle goes to about mid-scale, stop here and carefully adjust R_1. The sensitivity of this circuit will depend on the amount of power delivered to the dummy load and on the setting of R_1.

This circuit also provides a bit of a bonus. You can use it as a signal monitor. By substituting a small earphone for the multimeter, you will actually be able to hear the audio content of the signal from the transmitter. If single sideband is transmitted, all you'll get is a Donald Duck quacking, but with AM the audio quality should be quite clear.

OSCILLOSCOPE RF TEST PROBE

The oscilloscope is a useful device for visually displaying operating parameters of nearly every electronic circuit. However, if you try to connect one directly to an RF circuit, chances are you'll swamp this circuit and maybe even damage a component or two. For RF test purposes, a special probe is required which might cost $20 or more if you purchase a commercially made product. The circuit shown in Fig. 6-36 will cost less than $5 and will do the same thing. This is known as a shunt demodulator, and it does several things. First, it provides a high degree of isolation between the oscilloscope and the RF circuit. This prevents the RF energy from being swamped out. Second, this circuit rectifies or detects the RF signal and passes pulsating dc along to the scope's vertical input.

You will want to make this circuit as small as possible so that it will fit inside an existing test probe. You can often find these in surplus warehouses costing less than $1. The probe typically contains a plastic case, a ground strap, and a sharp metal point. One of these assemblies is used for another project in this book. I used point-to-point wiring to build this circuit, but it can be installed as easily on a tiny section of perf board. This board should be no more than $\frac{1}{2}$ in. wide but can be several inches long, owing to the length of the probe. All components are installed on the circuit board in close proximity to each other. D_1 and R_1 are tied together at their ground points and connected to the ground clip lead if one is provided. If not, use a piece of coaxial cable with the braid serving as ground. Install C_1 and D_1 as close to the probe tip as possible. When the circuit board is complete, insert the entire device in the barrel of the probe and connect the output of C_1 directly to the tip. Your circuit is now complete.

To use the probe, connect its output (shielded cable) to the scope vertical input and ground. Connect the ground clip wire to the RF circuit's ground and use the probe tip to access the various RF points. There you have it, a $20 probe for less than $5.

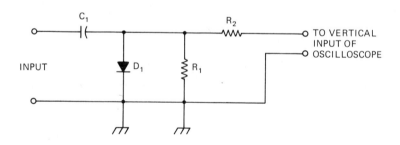

C_1 : 220 pF

D_1 : SK3087 (RCA)

R_1 : 100 kΩ, $\frac{1}{2}$ W CARBON

R_2 : 200 kΩ, $\frac{1}{2}$ W CARBON

FIGURE 6-36 Oscilloscope RF test probe.

AC-DC VOLTMETER

When performing electrical measurements, it is often necessary to switch the multimeter from dc operation to ac. This can be a hassle if you're deeply involved in a circuit and have just located the tiny contact points within a multitude of similar-looking contacts. First, you have to take your eyes away from the circuit and then switch to the ac position. Upon returning to the circuit, you may have to search for those same contacts which suddenly seem to have disappeared.

If the measurements you're making are not especially critical, the circuit shown in Fig. 6-37 may be just what you're looking for. It uses a dc voltmeter but will also take ac readings due to the four rectifiers which are placed across its inputs. When taking dc measurements, you don't have to worry about polarity either. This device will read both negative- and positive-going voltages, regardless of how the probes are connected to the voltage source.

This circuit is basically a full-wave bridge rectifier whose output terminals have been connected to the dc voltmeter's contacts. Polarity is observed at this point in construction, but its actual use requires no such attention. For example, when taking a dc voltage measurement in a circuit with a negative ground, it makes no difference which

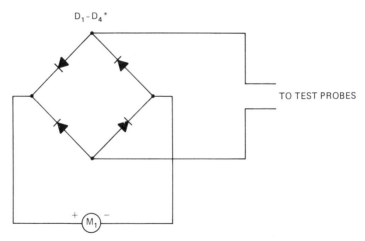

D_1-D_4: 800 PIV, 1 A (CURRENT RATING NOT IMPORTANT)

M_1: DC VOLTMETER

* PRV RATING SHOULD BE 20% HIGHER THAN MAXIMUM METER SCALE READING.

FIGURE 6-37 Ac-dc voltmeter.

probe is grounded and which is connected to the positive source. The same holds true for circuits with negative grounds. If you want to take an ac measurement, simply connect the probes.

This meter will read dc and rms voltage values, but due to the inclusion of the rectifiers, which introduce a slight voltage drop (usually 2 V or less), the readings will not be exactly precise. In most instances, you can add $1\frac{1}{2}$ or 2 V to what the meter indicates and come up with a close approximation of the true value. This circuit is most useful for measuring values of 50 V or more, since the 2-V drop becomes less of an overall percentage of the sum.

No meter is specified in the schematic diagram, as any type which is manufactured to read dc voltage will work. The circuit I built used a 0–150-V dc meter from Allied Electronics (Model 701-7115). It is useful for taking measurements down to about 25 V ac-dc. I used junk box rectifiers, each rated at 800 PRV and 1 A. The current rating is unimportant, as the meter will draw a miniscule amount of power. Diodes rated at 50 PRV may be substituted if you intend to take measurements below 50 volts ac-dc.

While four discrete rectifiers are specified, I have used a solid-state bridge rectifier package to construct one of these meters. The bridge was connected directly to the meter terminals and probes run from its ac input. The back of the meter was then wrapped with electrical tape, avoiding the necessity of a circuit board and meter case. The same mounting arrangement could be accomplished using four discrete diodes, but the overall project would be a little more difficult mechanically.

Regardless of which type of rectifier assembly you use, make certain the positive and negative outputs are connected to the positive and negative meter terminals. This is the only attention you need pay to polarity. When you test your meter, if you find the needle burying itself at the zero end of the scale, you can be certain the meter has been improperly connected at the diode circuit output. Reversing the connections should solve the problem. Incidentally, if you plan to use this circuit to measure relatively low voltage values (15 V and less), you may be able to make some partial adjustments by offsetting the needle indicator by a volt or so using the pointer adjust screw. This may be of some help in providing you with more accurate readings within a limited voltage range.

LINE VOLTAGE METER

You can convert almost any microammeter or milliammeter into a fairly accurate ac voltmeter by adding a rectifier circuit and a series resistor. The trick here is in choosing the value of the series resistor so that a current flow through the meter will be equal to the value of the voltage. For example, if the ac line voltage is 115 V ac, you will want to choose a resistor which will cause a current of 115 mA or μA to flow (depending on the type of meter used).

You will be much better off by using a microammeter. The lower current requirements mean that a low-wattage resistor can be used. This will consume a minimal amount of power from the line.

The circuit is shown in Fig. 6-38. The output from the ac line is connected directly to a standard full-wave bridge rectifier. Note that there is no filter capacitor at the rectifier output. If one were included, it would charge to the peak ac value, which would be approximately 1.4 times the rms value. In most ac measurements, the latter value is the one sought.

The output from the rectifier assembly is connected to a microammeter through a series resistor. The resistor limits current flow and is chosen to pass in microamperes the equivalent of the line voltage. Using a 1-MΩ resistor as shown, current flow will be 115 μA at 115 V ac, 120 μA at 120 V ac, etc. There will be a slight voltage drop through the rectifiers, but this is usually tolerable at line voltage values. If you wish to shoot for more accuracy, you can replace R_1 with a 1.5-MΩ potentiometer. Make sure this is a linear taper variety. You can then adjust this control for maximum accuracy using a separate line meter for calibration purposes. You will probably want to choose a precision trimmer resistor which can be mounted directly to the meter terminals. These contacts will also serve as connecting points for the bridge rectifier assembly. You can use four separate diodes here, but construction will move along more quickly by using a single packaged rectifier assembly. The completed project can then be housed in a plastic or aluminum case. A small insulated screwdriver is used to adjust the variable resistor if this component is opted for. You may have a bit of difficulty locating a 1.5-MΩ trimmer,

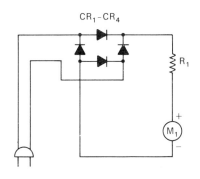

CR$_1$-CR$_4$: 1000 PIV, 1 A (BRIDGE ASSEMBLY)

M$_1$: 0–200 MICROAMPERES

FIGURE 6-38 Line voltage meter.   R$_1$: 1 MILLION Ω

but a 2-MΩ unit will do just about as well. Actually, the resistance value you end up with will be slightly less than 1 MΩ.

My circuit uses a surplus microammeter with a 0-200 scale. Other meter types may possess 0-150 scales, which are fine for measuring up to 150 V ac. If you have difficulty locating an appropriate microammeter, you can purchase one from Allied Electronics (Model 701-0015) for less than $20. Any microammeter, however, can be made to work, although you may have to design your own scale. It will be necessary to alter the series resistance accordingly. A 0-150 microammeter will require approximately 4 times the series resistance for a voltage indication at the same scale point.

When calculating the value of the series resistor, you simply divide the voltage by the current needed in amperes. For example, 115 V divided by .000115 A (115 μA) is 1 million Ω. This is the total series resistance needed to bring about a current flow of 115 μA at 115 V ac. You must also take into account the internal resistance of the meter, which will typically be somewhere around 600 Ω for a 0-200 microammeter. A fixed series resistor, then, would ideally be rated at 1 million Ω less 600 Ω. It will be necessary to subtract a little more resistance from this value to make up for the voltage drop across the rectifiers. This discussion is directed to those readers who must have extremely good accuracy. Since we're dealing with high resistance values, the meter's internal resistance can usually be discounted altogether. A circuit which reads exactly 115 μA at 115 V and uses a total series resistance (meter internal resistance and exterior resistance combined) will read 114.9 μA at 115 V ac when an additional 600 Ω of resistance is added to the circuit. This is a difference of only .1 V and probably can't even be seen on the meter.

Make certain the positive rectifier output is connected to the positive terminal of the meter (through R_1) and that the negative output connects to the negative terminal. If you find it more convenient to install the series resistor in the negative meter lead, the circuit will work just as well.

To test the circuit, simply insert the line plug into a wall outlet and note the reading. Using a 0-200 microammeter, the needle should point to approximately 115 μA. It's usually a good idea to test your meter with another line meter of known accuracy. In some areas line voltage will drop to 110 or so, while in other areas the line value can rise to nearly 130 V ac.

LED VOLTAGE INDICATOR

A simple voltage polarity indicator can be made by using a pair of reverse-connected light-emitting diodes (LEDs), as shown in Fig. 6-39. LEDs glow when they are forward biased, so one of the reverse-connected diodes will glow when the probes are connected in one polarity configuration. The other will glow when the probes are reversed. All you need to know is which diode indicates which test probe configuration. Simple circuits such as this have been used by hobbyists for years as a quick means of determining polarity at circuit points in electronic equipment. The series resistor is used to keep the voltage and current at values below the absolute maximum ratings of the LEDs.

Recently, a new device was offered which combines all the advantages of two LEDs in a single component. It's available from Radio Shack and is known as the Tri-Color Light-Emitting Diode (RS 276-035). This is a tristate light-emitting diode which will glow red, green, and yellow at different times based on the input polarity. It looks like any other LED and is connected in the same manner. It produces equal brightness at all three color outputs and will greatly simplify the previous circuit. It also adds a bit more versatility, which will be discussed later.

Figure 6-40 shows the circuit which uses the tricolor LED. Note that it eliminates the second diode altogether. This component has two leads, one short and one long. When a positive potential is connected to the short lead and a negative potential to the long one, the diode will glow green. When the test probes are reversed, the device will glow red. All you need do is think green for positive (at the short lead) and red for negative. The extra feature provided by this diode lies in the fact that it will glow yellow when connected to an alternating current source. In the previous circuit, both diodes would flicker with ac input. This serves as an electronic traffic light in that there are three possible indications: red, yellow, and green. Since red has long been associated with positive polarities (i.e., the positive test probes on most multimeters are colored red), I used the long lead of the LED for my reference and connected a probe with a red handle

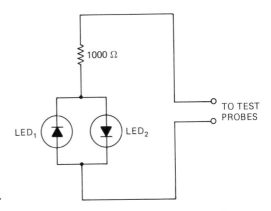

FIGURE 6-39 LED voltage indicator.

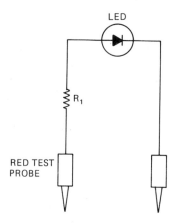

LED

R₁

RED TEST
PROBE

LED: RADIO SHACK 276-036

R_1 : 1000 Ω, $\frac{1}{2}$ W

FIGURE 6-40 LED voltage polarity indicator using a single diode.

to this point. The negative probe was connected to the short lead. In operation, if the diode glows red, I know my red probe is at a positive contact point. On the other hand, if the glow is green, this indicates that the red probe is connected to a negative point. A yellow glow is self-explanatory (alternating current). For my own personal use, I found this relationship of LED glow to probe coloration to be quite practical. You may not be so choosy, but it is mandatory to be able to distinguish between the two probes and to know which is connected to either of the two LED leads.

This circuit does have a drawback in that it is operational over a narrow voltage range. Using the 1000-Ω resistor specified, do not let probe voltage climb higher than a value of approximately 18 V dc. If you wish to use this circuit to indicate the polarity of higher potentials, you will have to increase the series resistor accordingly. When you double the measured maximum voltage, you will also have to double the ohmic value of R_1. This will set a lower limit on potentials which will cause the LED to glow.

You can mount this circuit in a small plastic enclosure, but this is really a waste of space and time. If you can locate a surplus test probe from an electronic multimeter, it will more than likely provide you with the mounting space needed inside its grip. Probes of this type often contain a separate ground connection which is simply clipped to the chassis or other ground point. The probe tip is then used to explore the circuit. I found it quite easy to drill a hole in the grip, through which to mount the LED. The series resistor was connected between the long LED lead and the probe tip. The probe ground lead was connected to the remaining LED lead, and I ended up with a completely self-contained test probe with no external wires

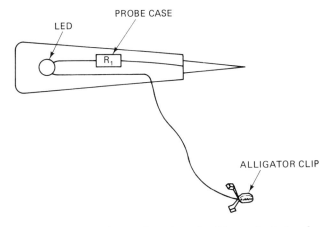

FIGURE 6-41 Installation of previous circuit in surplus test probe.

or cables, which would normally return to a multimeter. Figure 6-41 shows the circuit installation in the surplus test probe.

LOGIC INDICATOR LAMP DRIVER

A previous circuit used an optoisolator coupled to a triac in order to control an ac load. The circuit shown in Fig. 6-42 uses another GE optoisolator, the H11C1. Both components are quite similar, but the one used in this circuit involves an internal LED optically coupled to an LASCR instead of a triac. When the diode fires, the LASCR is triggered and conducts current from a 120-V ac line through an in-

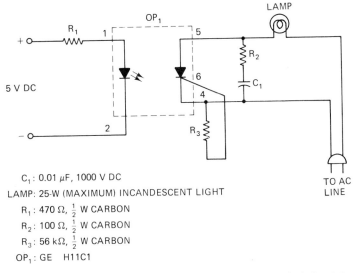

C$_1$: 0.01 μF, 1000 V DC
LAMP: 25-W (MAXIMUM) INCANDESCENT LIGHT
R$_1$: 470 Ω, $\frac{1}{2}$ W CARBON
R$_2$: 100 Ω, $\frac{1}{2}$ W CARBON
R$_3$: 56 kΩ, $\frac{1}{2}$ W CARBON
OP$_1$: GE   H11C1

FIGURE 6-42 Logic indicator lamp driver. (Courtesy General Electric.)

dicator lamp, also rated at 120 V ac. The lamp must be a small type, as current drain cannot exceed 300 mA. To play it safe, you should limit current to the lamp to about 200 mA, or about 25 W.

This circuit is designed to be driven from the 5-V dc output of a TTL or DTL logic circuit. The 470-Ω series resistor in the LED circuit limits current to about 20 mA, which is all that is required to activate the LED.

The H11C1 optoisolator is contained in a mini-DIP six-pin package and can probably be mounted in the compartment which houses the logic circuit. The output from pins 4 and 5 may be connected directly to the indicator lamp and the ac line. The gate circuit of the internal LASCR consists of a single 56-kΩ $\frac{1}{2}$-W resistor connected between pins 4 and 6. The output network consisting of the 100-Ω resistor and .1-μf capacitor is connected between pins 4 and 5, bridging the ac line. The circuit may be put together on a piece of perf board, as was the case with the previous optoisolator circuits. Just be sure the connections to pins 5 and 4 are made without any accidental solder bridges to the input circuit at pins 1 and 2. When correctly connected, the circuit offers the equivalent of 1500 V of isolation between input and output.

When the logic circuit fires, the internal LED is activated, causing the internal LASCR to conduct current. The line current then passes through the indicator lamp. The lamp will continue to glow until the logic input reverts to a zero state. The last statement is not exactly accurate from a theoretical standpoint. Actually, the LASCR will continue to conduct current even when the logic input is removed and will not shut down until the ac voltage returns to zero. Alternating current swings from positive to negative 60 times/s and thus returns to zero with each transition. For the LASCR to switch off instantaneously, the logic input signal must be removed at a time during which the ac cycle is going from positive to negative or vice versa. If the input signal is removed at the start of a half cycle, the lamp will glow until that half cycle is complete. This, however, would occur within a very small fraction of a second, so from a practical standpoint, we can say that the lamp goes off when the input voltage is removed.

LED AUDIO POWER METER

In some measurement applications, it is desirable to have a visual readout of circuit conditions. This is what basic meters are all about. However, sometimes logarithmic (mechanical) and even digital meters are not the most appropriate devices for these indications. In recent years, several integrated circuits have been designed which will directly drive light-emitting diodes. The latter components are arranged in a line which forms a type of bar graph or bar meter. When used for voltage measurements, the illumination of one diode indicates a certain specific voltage. When two are activated, this may indicate twice the value. This type of meter requires that simple extrapolation be used by the operator to obtain the proper reading. As long as the person using the device knows which value each LED indicates, the circuit can be quite valuable in indicating many different electronic parameters. These types of metering devices are usually not as accurate as mechanical or digital readout meters, but for many applications a bar display will serve a very useful purpose.

Commercial audio power meters can be quite expensive, especially if you want high accuracy. For most stereo buffs and electronic experimenters, however, a general indication of output is all that is required. The circuit shown in Fig. 6-43 does not use expensive meters and is quite simple to attach in parallel with a speaker to provide a step indication of approximate audio power output. The circuit uses the National Semiconductor LM3915, which is an 18-pin DIP chip. This is a monolithic integrated circuit that senses analog voltage levels and will drive 10 light-emitting diodes, providing a logarithmic

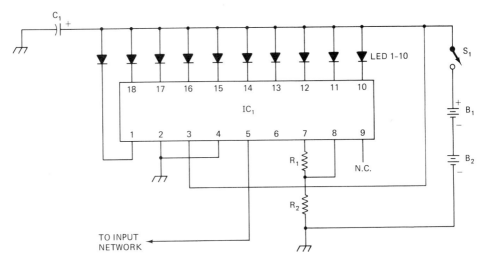

B_1-B_2: 9 V TRANSISTOR RADIO TYPE

C_1: 2.2 μF MINIATURE ELECTROLYTIC (ALLIED ELECTRONICS 852-5663)

LED 1-10: 10 RED LIGHT EMITTING DIODES OR 10 DIODE ARRAY

IC_1: LM3915 (NATIONAL SEMICONDUCTOR)

R_1: 390 Ω, $\frac{1}{2}$ W CARBON

R_2: 2.7 kΩ, $\frac{1}{2}$ W CARBON

S_1: SPST MINIATURE

FIGURE 6-43   LED audio power meter. (Courtesy National Semiconductor.)

3-dB/step analog display. The IC contains an adjustable voltage reference and a highly accurate 10-step voltage divider. The high-impedance input buffer accepts signals down to ground and up to within 1.5 V of the positive supply potential. This particular circuit will operate from a potential as low as 12 V dc up to about 20 V dc. For practical applications, I've used a power supply which consists of two 9-V batteries wired in series to deliver 18 V dc between the $V+$ IC connection and the LED string.

The integrated circuit is slightly under 1 in. long and a little over $\frac{1}{4}$ in. wide. I do not recommend that you solder the various component leads directly to the IC pins. It is much simpler to mount an 18-pin IC socket in the center of a 4- by 4-in. circuit board, make all connections, and snap the IC into place. This IC is quite versatile and can be used for many other applications, so the socket allows you to easily make circuit changes without the fear of damaging the LM3915 due to soldering iron heat.

Once the socket has been installed, the 10 red LEDs should be soldered in place. Be sure the cathodes of each are connected to the socket pin leads, while the anodes are connected in parallel and grounded through a 2.2-μF electrolytic capacitor. Once this wiring is complete, the major portion of the work is done. Only a few additional components are needed to complete the circuit. At pin 7 (the reference output), the 390-Ω $\frac{1}{2}$-W carbon resistor is soldered in place with its opposite lead connected to pin 8. Short out pins 6 and 7 with a small jumper composed of insulated hookup wire. A 2.7-kΩ resistor of the same composition and wattage value is connected between pins 8 and 4 of the IC socket. Pin 2 is also shorted to pin 4, which provides grounding for the two pins. Pin 9 is not used in this configuration.

The only pin remaining unused is the signal input (pin 5). This is used to make connection to the output amplifier whose power is to be measured. This is accomplished through a voltage divider network which you may wish to install directly at the speaker or which can also be contained on the audio power meter circuit board. In the latter configuration, two output leads will be clipped directly to the speaker terminals. Figure 6-44 shows the voltage divider network consisting of two $\frac{1}{2}$-W carbon resistors. R_3 will always be 10 Ω, but R_4 is changed to reflect the load impedance. Some amplifiers are designed to deliver full power into a load impedance of 4, 8, or 16 Ω. Eight ohms would seem to be the most common output impedance, but this may vary from manufacturer to manufacturer. The easiest way to check the impedance of your amplifier's output is to consult the technical operations guide, but if this is no help, simply gain access to the speaker(s) in the audio unit whose power is to be measured. You will generally find the impedance value printed on the speaker

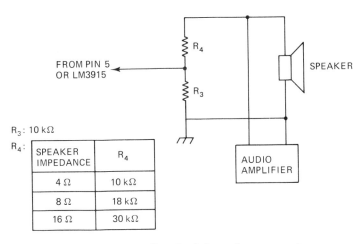

R$_3$: 10 kΩ

R$_4$:

SPEAKER IMPEDANCE	R$_4$
4 Ω	10 kΩ
8 Ω	18 kΩ
16 Ω	30 kΩ

FIGURE 6-44 Sampling circuit for audio power meter.

magnet. A 4-Ω amplifier output means that R_4 will be of a 10-kΩ value, 8 Ω requires an 18-kΩ resistor, while a 16-Ω output will require R_4 to be rated at 30 kΩ.

Notice that the bottom of R_3 is connected directly to pin 2 of the IC, this being the circuit ground. If you wish to have the capability of measuring the audio output of several different types of equipment, you may wish to add a three-position rotary switch to the circuit. This would be used to switch in any one of the three different $\frac{1}{2}$-W carbon resistors used for R_4 when impedance changes. This will serve to make the circuit more versatile.

Before installing the IC in its socket, examine the circuit carefully. This is a tiny 18-pin package, and it's quite easy to accidentally mistake one pin for another. This type of mistake could cause the IC to be destroyed when power is applied. Once you are satisfied that the IC has been wired properly, check your string of light-emitting diodes once again, making certain the cathode of each is connected to an appropriate IC socket pin. Check C_1 to make certain it is connected with its positive lead attached to the common anode of the 10 LEDs. As a final check, make certain all the IC pins have been utilized, with the exception of pin 9. If you find more than one vacant pin, a wiring error has occurred, and it will be necessary to correct the situation before proceeding further.

When you are certain the circuit is complete, install the LM3915. *Caution:* The IC will fit perfectly in the socket in two different ways. Make certain pin 1 of the IC is in pin 1 of the IC socket. A reversal here would place IC pin 10 in the number 1 socket pin position, which will lead to disaster. The oval identifier at one end of the LM3915 should be pointed toward the left of the IC socket when aligned to match the schematic.

Two 9-V batteries are now connected to their terminal strips. Make certain you have a true series connection by measuring the output. It should read approximately 18 V dc. Double-check your connections between the battery pack, the switch, and the IC to be sure correct polarity has been observed. The positive output from the batteries is connected to pin 3 of the IC through the SPST switch.

It's time to test your circuit, so with power off, clip the leads from the voltage divider to the speaker contacts of your audio device. Activate S_1 and activate the audio amplifier. Depending on the output of the amplifier, you may note that the first five or six LEDs glow immediately. If not, increase the power by advancing the volume control. As explained earlier, each LED represents a 3-dB increase in power, with LED 1 glowing at a level of .2 W. Power output must be doubled in order to cause LED 2 to glow. LED 3 will glow when the power level of the previous step is doubled. By using the step metering technique, power indications of levels up to 100 W can be read with this solid-step meter circuit. From a practical standpoint, the upper levels of this device's range tell you less and less about the exact power output level. For example, if LED 8 glows but LED 9 does not, this simply means that your amplifier is producing an output power of at least 25 W but less than 50 W. The true power output could be anywhere from 26 to 49 W. If you have an amplifier which is rated to deliver 50 W of power and LED 9 will not glow, this is a good indication that your amplifier is not producing what it's supposed to.

This circuit is designed for portable operation and is built using separate LEDs. You can modify this circuit by going with an LED array, and you can even build an ac-derived dc power supply for a fixed installation, where portable operation offered by the battery pack is not desirable. It won't take the place of a precision audio wattmeter for more exacting measurement of audio amplifier power, but it does make a handy test instrument that doesn't require all the adjustments a highly complex circuit would. For stereo amplifiers, you may wish to build two of these circuits, one for each channel. Due to the size of the overall circuit, you should be able to incorporate it in an existing stereo unit. My circuit was not enclosed in a typical plastic or aluminum box due to the fact that the LEDs were mounted directly to the circuit board surface. Of course, an enclosure arrangement could be used by mounting the LEDs to an external terminal strip. This circuit offers many modifications and mounting configurations which can be tailored to suit individual preference.

LED VU METER

Figure 6-45 shows a circuit which is very similar to the one previously presented but uses the LM3916 dot-bar display driver from National Semiconductor. When completed, the circuit will serve as a VU meter and will contain no moving parts, as is the case with standard logarithmic meters. The IC contains an adjustable voltage reference and an accurate 10-step voltage divider. The high-impedance input buffer accepts signals to within 1.5 V of the positive supply (12 to 20 V).

When completed as shown, the circuit is a fast-responding electronic VU meter which may be contained in a very small package. Construction is nearly identical to the previous project in regard to the chip and the LEDs. Two supplies will be required with this project. One will deliver 12 to 20 V dc between pin 3 and ground, while the other will drive the LEDs and should supply 3 V (positive). The signal source is connected at pins 4 and 5. Note that C_1 is required only when the LED display is mounted some distance from the chip. You can get away with leads to pins 10-18 and to pin 1 of just under 6 in., but past this point, C_1 is required. When a single diode is lit based on drive from the signal source, this is an indication that the input level is 20 dB below zero. As is customary with logarithmic meters, this device will provide indications to +3 dB.

AUDIO LIMITER

Shortwave listeners who often tune for hours on end, trying to detect those rare stations, have more than once been nearly floored by a sudden loud signal on the same frequency. This occurs when audio volume is increased to try and pick up the weak stations and a much stronger station suddenly comes on the air. During these listening periods, headphones are almost always worn, and the ear-splitting volume is startling and painful. The same thing can occur when a thunderstorm moves into the general vicinity, accompanied by the high-amplitude cracks which are transmitted during every lightning flash.

The circuit shown in Fig. 6-46 will eliminate much of this problem. It uses two common silicon diodes to limit the amount of signal which can pass on to the headphones. Below a certain amplitude, the diodes act as if they were not even in the circuit, but during a sudden volume increase, they conduct and short out most of the signal.

If you use $\frac{1}{4}$-W resistors instead of the $\frac{1}{2}$-W components specified, you can probably install the entire circuit inside a large phone plug

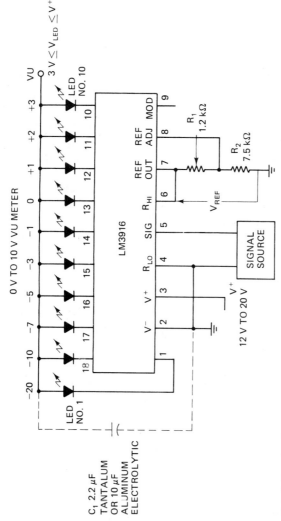

FIGURE 6-45 LED VU meter. (Courtesy National Semiconductor.)

Note 1: Capacitor C_1 is required if leads to the LED supply are 6 in. or longer.

Note 2: Circuit as shown is wired for dot mode. For bar mode, connect pen 9 to pen 3. V_{LED} must be kept below 7 V or dropping resistor should be used to limit IC power dissipation.

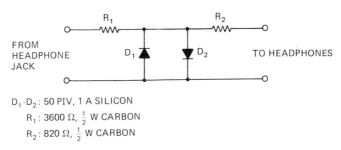

D_1-D_2: 50 PIV, 1 A SILICON

R_1: 3600 Ω, $\frac{1}{2}$ W CARBON

R_2: 820 Ω, $\frac{1}{2}$ W CARBON

FIGURE 6-46 Simple audio limiter.

housing. This circuit is not critical at all. I used a couple of junk box diodes which were rated at 50 PIV, but most other types will work as well. Higher PIV ratings may bring about a slight increase in overall volume. Make certain the diodes are reverse connected (in relationship to each other), as shown in the schematic diagram. The circuit requires no adjustments, as the limiting feature is automatic. When installed between your receiver and headphones, this circuit will limit the maximum volume that can be obtained. For the really weak stations, this may be a bit of a problem, but most of the time you can listen intently to signals without being in constant fear of having your eardrums shattered by a lightning flash or super-powerful station.

DIODE NOISE GENERATOR

Have you ever been in a situation where it was necessary to tune a receiver for maximum sensitivity by using an on-the-air signal? This can be quite a nuisance at times, since signals tend to fade and transmission seems to stop right at the critical portion of your alignment. If you're fortunate, your shop is equipped with an RF signal generator which will give you a steady input to the receiver, avoiding all these problems. Sometimes, however, it's not always possible to make an alignment at your workbench, and portable RF signal generators can be quite expensive.

The circuit shown in Fig. 6-47 is self-contained and can be carried with you almost anywhere you go. It's so simple that it can be put together within an hour's time and does a pretty fair job in less-than-ideal alignment situations. This is not an RF signal generator in the sense that you know it. I call it my electronic vacuum cleaner because it's really a noise generator and produces much the same conditions at a receiver as my vacuum cleaner motor does when it's operating. This circuit produces an output which is detected as a hissing sound at the receiver speaker. The noise which is generated

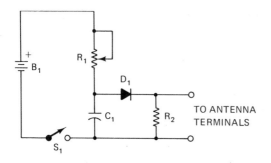

B$_1$: 9 V

C$_1$: 500 pF DISK

D$_1$: RADIO SHACK 276–1124

R$_1$: 50 kΩ, $\frac{1}{2}$ W (LINEAR TAPER)

R$_2$: 50 Ω, $\frac{1}{2}$ W CARBON

S$_1$: SPST

FIGURE 6-47 Diode noise generator.

covers a very broad frequency range, so this device can be used for alignment of all high-frequency receivers. It won't tell you a thing about adjacent channel rejection, since its output frequency is so broad, but it does generate enough noise to peak the receiver RF amplifier for maximum noise heard at the speaker. As shown, the circuit has a good output, even into the VHF spectrum, although I have not used it for aligning this type of equipment. The output is terminated in a 50-Ω resistor to match the input impedance of most modern receivers. For communications receivers designed to accept a long wire antenna, try a higher value for better results. R_1 controls the noise level. Most of the time this will be set at the midrange position and left in place while you observe the receiver S-meter to determine when sensitivity is increased by your adjustments. If the noise level becomes too high, simply back off on R_1.

I built my entire circuit on a 4-in. square section of perf board, mounting S_1 and R_1 here using miniature printed circuit board components. Most of the time, however, these circuits are installed in a plastic or aluminum case with the variable components mounted through the enclosure walls. The circuit is fairly noncritical. Just make certain you observe polarity at D_1 and at the diode. I originally built this circuit over 15 years ago and used a 1N21 diode as the noise generator. This is a specialized diode and is rather hard to cross-reference in today's catalogs. I did find a direct replacement, however, from Radio Shack. Do not substitute common germanium diodes for this device, as they will not work. While I have not tried the Radio Shack replacement, I have been assured that it is an exact replacement, and it should work fine in your circuit.

When your circuit is complete, connect the output terminals to the input of your receiver and turn on both units. Adjust R_1 until a steady hiss is heard. You are now in a position to align the front end (RF amplifier) of your receiver, making adjustments for a maximum S-meter reading or the loudest signal at the speaker.

AC MOTOR BRAKE

A motor which is designed to work only from alternating current will act just like a short circuit if direct current is applied. Therefore, one must always be careful never to accidentally use direct current in an attempt to operate such motors. In situations where this occurs, the dc power supply may be destroyed. More often, however, the fuse is simply blown, and no permanent damage results. In cases where the dc power supply is capable of delivering extremely high currents, the ac motor is damaged. When dc current enters the motor winding, it begins to heat up, and permanent winding damage can occur within a very short period of time. A fire hazard is present, since the insulation around the windings usually burns, producing a black, acrid smoke.

The reason for this explanation is due to the circuit that will be discussed here, which will result in a means of instantly stopping the rotation of an ac motor. This is accomplished by applying direct current to the windings, and you must be sure to wire the circuit correctly. Fortunately, however, the circuit shown in Fig. 6-48 provides only a short burst of dc current, so we don't get into the undesirable aspects of this practice. When dc current is applied to an ac motor which is operational, the rotating shaft suddenly freezes. A high amount of current is drawn as long as the current is applied, so the circuit is fitted with a spring-loaded switch that automatically returns to the on position shortly after it's depressed. With the return, the diode is removed from the circuit.

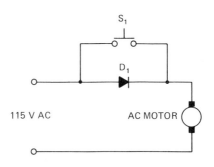

D_1: 200 PIV, 10 A

S_1: NORMALLY CLOSED MOMENTARY
SWITCH (CONTACTS RATED 20% HIGHER
THAN MAXIMUM MOTOR CURRENT)

FIGURE 6-48 **Motor brake circuit.**

The circuit consists of a single diode rectifier and the momentary switch, a normally closed type. The switch is wired in parallel with the diode and effectively shorts this component out, so that alternating current is always fed to the motor until the switch is activated. When the switch is depressed, its contacts open, and current passes through the diode, where it is rectified, producing a dc input at the motor. All that is necessary is to simply "hit" the switch and then immediately remove your finger to allow it to return to the closed position. The short burst of direct current will stop the motor's rotation. When the switch springs back to the closed position, ac is once again applied to the windings, and operation begins.

A motor brake circuit of this type is most often used as a means of stopping rotation during an emergency situation. This could occur when the motor linkage becomes defective and the equipment it powers begins shaking apart. Here the momentary switch will be depressed with one hand, while the other hand is actively involved in cutting ac power to prevent the motor from starting up again.

The components specified for this circuit can serve as guidelines to building your own. Since a high amount of current will be drawn, the rectifier should be rated at 10 times the normal operating current of the motor. The switch contact will pass the normal operating current and should be rated 20% higher than the maximum current which is likely to be drawn by the motor. I have never used this circuit with the larger motors due to the high amounts of current they draw under normal operating conditions, but if you use a big enough diode rectifier, any ac motor can be controlled with this circuit.

Most of the high-amperage rectifiers require a fairly large heat sink in order to be operated at their maximum ratings. In most instances, this will not be necessary due to the short time the device is in the circuit. While a high amount of current will be drawn, this will occur for only a fraction of a second, so the case does not have time to heat past absolute maximum ratings.

While I have never experienced any problem with fuses blowing while using this circuit, if your primary line is operating near maximum output, you may have difficulties. The primary circuit must be fused, but a slow-blow type should provide you with adequate protection and will not respond quite so quickly to the instantaneous surge that occurs when the momentary switch is depressed.

There are many different ways of installing this circuit, but I chose to enclose mine in a small aluminum box which was equipped with a power cord (to access the 115-V ac line). At the other end of the box, there is a female receptacle which supplies power to the motor. My diode was installed directly across the switch contacts. A pictorial drawing of my setup is shown in Fig. 6-49. While the primary line is fused, the fuse contained in this device provides a secondary

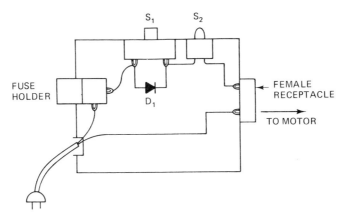

FIGURE 6-49 Enclosure wiring for brake circuit.

backup. For my purposes, a 20-A buss fuse was more than adequate. Note that a second switch (S_2) has been installed in the aluminum box as well. This cuts all power to the motor. My practice is to hit S_1, which applies dc to the motor windings, and then to immediately switch S_2 to the off position. This keeps the motor from starting up again. Only the basic circuit is presented in the schematic diagram. It can be altered to suit your individual operating needs. The connection of D_1 in the circuit may be reversed from that shown, as the polarity of the direct current delivered to the motor is unimportant. As shown in the schematic diagram, the output from the rectifier is positive. A reversal of the diode would result in a negative output. Either way, the motor shaft will stop turning.

VOLTAGE DOUBLER ADD-ON CIRCUIT

Commercially manufactured power supplies are often quite expensive, and the resourceful home experimenter often overcomes this problem by building these devices at home. One of the mainstays of the home power supply builder is the television power transformer. Every day, thousands upon thousands of junked color and black and white television receivers are hauled to the dump. This is a shame, because many of these seemingly useless devices offer a wealth of electronic components which might cost several hundred dollars if purchased new. Since my teenage years, I have been picking up scrap television receivers, removing the useful components and then hauling them away myself. Most TV repair facilities are more than happy to have experimenters do this, as it saves them the expense that hauling away always entails.

The older black and white television receivers (especially the console models) are equipped with very rugged power transformers. These may be rated for a continuous duty operation of 300 W or more, and when called to intermittent service such as that involved in amateur transmitters and other electronic projects, they can easily be pushed to twice this power output without exceeding their continuous commercial service ratings.

These old transformers usually operated into vacuum tube rectifiers which required a 5-V ac filament voltage. When converted for modern power supply applications, however, this winding is not needed, and the leads may be simply clipped away. However, with the add-on voltage doubler circuit shown in Fig. 6-50, you can use this 5-V winding to produce an output of up to 14 V dc. Under a bit of a load, this value will drop closer to 12 V, which can be used to drive many different circuits. The voltage doubler shown provides reasonably good dynamic regulation, but this can be improved upon by providing a zener diode regulator or even a more sophisticated IC voltage regulator circuit. As shown, the circuit may be used with ac inputs of up to approximately 30 V. It is designed to produce a maximum output of just under 100 V dc but will operate quite nicely at much lower potentials.

The entire circuit is installed on a single section of perforated circuit board which may be later mounted in an existing power supply enclosure. The peak output voltage will be equal to approximately 2.8 times the rms value. Voltage doubler circuits provide twice the peak ac value at their outputs. A transformer with a 5-V winding really produces nearly 7 V peak. The 5-V value is an average and is what you would measure with a standard ac voltmeter.

Figure 6-51 shows a suggested component layout on the circuit board. Make certain you don't reverse the connections of D_1 and D_2,

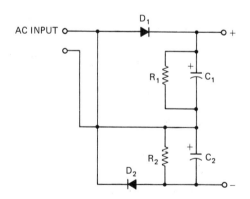

C$_1$-C$_2$: 500 μF 100 V DC

D$_1$-D$_2$: 100 PIV, 1 A

R$_1$-R$_2$: 15 kΩ, 1 W

FIGURE 6-50   Line-driven full-wave voltage doubler.

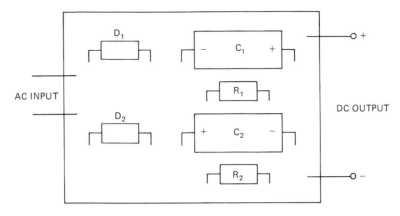

FIGURE 6-51 Voltage doubler circuit layout.

as this will render the power supply useless. Also, note the connection between C_1 and C_2. The negative terminal of C_1 is connected to the positive terminal of C_2. This is actually a series connection of two electrolytic capacitors. During one portion of the ac cycle, D_1 charges C_1 to nearly 7 V. During the next half cycle, D_2 charges C_2 to the same potential. When capacitors are series connected in a voltage doubler circuit, their charged values add, so the peak output will be nearly 14 V dc.

Two bleeder resistors are connected in the circuit to discharge C_1 and C_2 when the supply is deactivated. Without them, the unloaded power supply potential would remain long after primary power had been cut. These resistors also serve another purpose, that of component matching. The two filter capacitors should be of the same value and made by the same manufacturer. Even then, there will be very minute differences in the two, and one could charge to a much higher value than the other. This could cause the one which drops the most voltage to exceed its maximum ratings if the power supply was operated close to its maximum output. The parallel-connected bleeder resistors minimize internal resistance differences and cause each capacitor to drop the same amount or one-half of the total output voltage.

To operate this circuit, simply connect the transformer output leads to the input. With a dc voltmeter at the output of the doubler, you should measure a value approximately equal to 2.8 times the rms or measured dc value at the input. If you experience problems, it's more than likely due to a reversed diode or capacitor or other such wiring error. While a 5-V ac input will yield nearly 14 V peak, you may wish to connect your circuit to a winding with a higher or lower ac output. Some transformers may even offer a 5-V center-tapped winding which will measure 2.5 V either side of the center tap. By using the center tap and only one side of that particular winding for a 2.5-V ac input, the voltage doubler will deliver a peak dc output of nearly 7 V. A 6.3-V input will yield 17.5 V, while a 12.6-V input will give you a dc output of about 33 V. Remember, these are peak values and will drop a bit when current is drawn. The diodes used in this circuit allow a maximum current drain of just under 1 A, allowing a bit for component safety purposes, but this does not necessarily mean that you can draw the entire amount. The current rating of the transformer secondary will be a determining factor. For example, if a winding were rated at 1 A, you could draw only half this amount in a voltage doubler circuit. While the voltage is doubled, the current must be halved. A drain of 500 mA ($\frac{1}{2}$ A) from a voltage doubler circuit results in a current drain at the transformer winding of twice this amount, or 1 A. Keep this in mind when designing your power supply to avoid operating the transformer in excess of its maximum rating.

TRANSFORMERLESS POWER SUPPLY

Most dc power supplies which derive their input from the 115-V ac line use a power transformer to step the voltage up or down in order for rectification to take place at a value which is more in line with the desired output. Power transformers are often the most expensive power supply circuit components. They also add appreciably to the overall size and weight of the finished unit. In some applications, however, the transformer may be done away with completely. These are known as transformerless power supplies, and several decades ago they were quite popular. Today, however, the transformerless power supply is very rarely used, although it does have several advantages. Such supplies can often be fitted into existing equipment due to their small relative size, and most can be built for a fraction of the cost of a similar supply which uses a transformer.

Figure 6-52 shows a circuit for a power supply which will deliver a peak dc output of 160 V. Under a 500-mA load, however, the output will drop to a value of approximately 150 V. This circuit is identical in most ways to many other power supplies in that a bridge rectifier is incorporated, along with a filter capacitor and bleeder resistor. The only difference is that the transformer is missing. The 115-V ac potential from the line is connected to the input of the full-wave bridge circuit, where it is rectified. C_1 is a 100-μF filter capacitor, which smooths out the ac ripple and produces a pure dc output. R_1 places a minimum load on the power supply output and discharges the capacitor when the circuit is switched off.

Figure 6-53 shows a suggested component layout on a section of perforated circuit board. Note that the fuse is installed here as well. This can be accomplished by purchasing a 2-A fuse which has

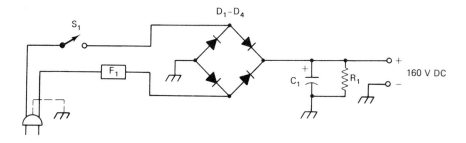

C₁: 100 μF   250 V DC
D₁-D₄: 500 PIV , 1 A
F₁: 2 A
R₁: 50 kΩ, 2 W CARBON
S₁: SPST 3 A

FIGURE 6-52 Transformerless power supply.

already been fitted with wire leads. Alternately, a small circuit board fuseholder may be used to facilitate replacement.

If this circuit is to be mounted in a separate enclosure, choose a small aluminum box which is drilled to accept the toggle switch. You will also want to install an output terminal strip, the ground size of which is attached directly to the aluminum case. Small-diameter $1\frac{1}{2}$-in. bolts fitted with spacers and matching nuts are placed through the bottom of the enclosure to keep the circuit board out of reach of a potential short circuit. Insulated hookup wiring connects the switch to its circuit board contacts. Small holes should be drilled in the back panel of the case and fitted with rubber grommets to prevent cutting of the insulation on the three-conductor cable.

To test the circuit, make certain S_1 is in the off position and in-

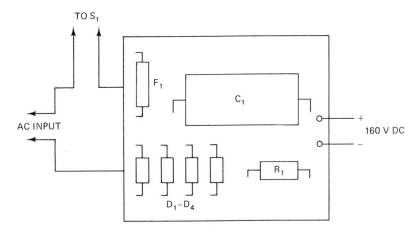

FIGURE 6-53 Component layout for previous circuit.

sert the line plug in a wall receptacle. Connect the probes of a dc volt-meter across the output terminals of this power supply. (Observe polarity.) Now activate S_1 and note the meter reading. You should get approximately 160 V, possibly a little more or a little less. If you get no output, remove the line plug from the wall and check the fuse. If this has opened up, there is probably a wiring error or short circuit between the perf board components and the case. This may be evidenced by a carbon buildup on the case created by the arc. Correct these situations, replace the fuse, and try again.

While this circuit was designed for 115-V ac operation, you can double your output voltage simply by replacing C_1 with a 100-μF electrolytic capacitor rated at 450 V dc and operating from a 230-V line. The output will now be close to 320 V dc. The amount of current which may be drawn using 115 or 230 V ac should be held to about 800 mA. This provides an adequate safety margin to protect the 1-A rectifiers. This means you can operate into loads of up to 90 W at 115 V or 180 W with the higher input potential. If you need to increase power capability, replace D_1-D_4 with 2- or 3-A units.

One of the reasons for the unpopularity of the transformerless power supply lies in the fact that half-wave circuits were often used. This grounds one side of the ac line to the case. I'm not speaking here of the ground pin connection used in the circuit presented but of one of the two outputs at the wall receptacle. If the plug is not connected to the output properly in these earlier cases, the full line potential will be present between the case and any other device connected to the ac line and grounded to it. Some transformerless supplies used half-wave voltage multiplier circuits with dc outputs of 750 V or more. A plug reversal here could cause a lethal potential to be present between the power supply case and other grounded devices.

The circuit in this project uses a full-wave rectifier, and there is no direct connection between the ac line and the case. I feel a full-wave transformerless power supply is the only type which should be built today. It can be safely used without undue fear of electric shock.

INSTANT-OFF POWER SUPPLY

Chances are you've noticed that when you turn off a radio, stereo, or any other type of device operated from a dc power supply it still continues to operate for $\frac{1}{2}$ s or so. Audio devices will sometimes output a popping or cracking sound. You can blame this on the power supply, which is not defective but operating as it is designed to. When you remove primary power from the supply, the filter capacitors are still charged to the full dc potential. It takes a short while for them to discharge, so full voltage and current are still delivered to the load while this is taking place. Power supplies with solid-state regulators often do not exhibit these properties, or at least not to the degree an unregulated supply does. While the problems created by this discharge are very minor, they can be squelched completely with the circuit shown in Fig. 6-54. This is an instant-off power supply which uses a reverse-connected diode in the negative or positive output lead (negative shown in the schematic) to block the flow of direct current. This is a switched arrangement using a DPDT device which cuts ac power and inserts the diode in the circuit through a single action. The reverse-connected diode will not conduct current, and the load is disconnected from the dc output at the same time primary power is removed from the transformer. This will end your bleed-off problems forever.

During normal operation, D_1 is shorted out by one section of S_1. When the switch is open, the short is removed, and dc is placed in series with the power supply and load in the reverse-biased mode. D_1 can be any silicon diode with a PIV rating slightly higher than the maximum dc output voltage.

Actually, you can remove the diode completely and leave a break at the point where it was connected, and dc power will still be removed when the supply is deactivated. However, installing a switch directly in the dc line could induce transients upon activation. This circuit can be installed in existing power supplies with very little difficulty. S_1 can be installed in the position occupied by the existing power switch. Make certain you get your connections

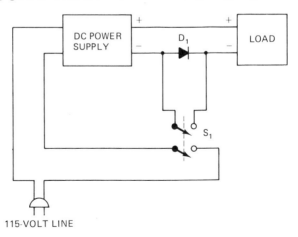

115-VOLT LINE

D_1 : ANY SILICON DIODE RATED HIGHER THAN
   THE DC OUTPUT VOLTAGE AND CURRENT
S_1 : DPDT SWITCH

FIGURE 6-54   Instant-off power supply.

right, or you might connect the load directly to one side of the ac line. Be sure your existing supply is equipped with bleeder resistors across the filter capacitors. Many inexpensive supplies forego this and depend on the load to bleed off the stored power, which is what this circuit is supposed to prevent.

POWER SUPPLY WITH INTERRUPT PROTECTION

Through the use of solid-state diodes, ac-derived power supplies are quite compact and relatively inexpensive to build. When you depend on the ac line to provide a dc output through these supplies, you never have to worry about battery replacement, and a great deal of expense can be avoided. However, ac power has been known to fail, and there you are with no dc output to power your electronic projects. A power outage can be especially disastrous when ac-derived power supplies are used to power memory circuits which must have operating current in order to retain what has been input.

The circuit shown in Fig. 6-55 is a simple zener diode-regulated dc power supply much like many of the other regulated supplies discussed in this chapter. This one, however, will protect power-dependent loads in the event that you experience an ac power failure. In most instances, it will also protect the load from a failure within the power supply itself, such as a popped rectifier or a zener diode.

Since regulated power supplies have been discussed previously,

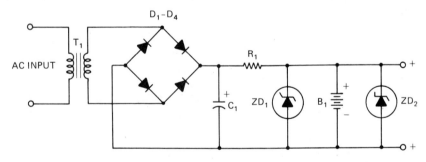

B$_1$: 9-V RECHARGEABLE BATTERY

C$_1$: 500 μF, 25 V DC

D$_1$-D$_4$: 50 PIV, 1 A

R$_1$: 50 Ω, 5 W

T$_1$: 115 V PRIMARY   12 V SECONDARY (200 MA OR GREATER)

ZD$_1$: 9.1-V ZENER DIODE 1 W

ZD$_2$: SAME AS ZD$_1$ (OPTIONAL)

FIGURE 6-55   Interrupt protection power supply circuit.

150 Solid-State Diode Projects

it is not necessary to go into the complete construction of this supply. Rather, we shall deal with the single component which provides the backup power source. This is a 9-V rechargeable battery which is connected across the output terminal. When the power supply is operating normally, this battery receives a constant charge. A fully charged battery will require only a minimal amount of current, or none at all. But should the power supply fail for any reason, the battery takes over fully and provides power to the load with no interruption whatsoever. In effect, the battery and power supply operate in parallel, but when the power supply is inactive, the battery takes over alone. For this reason, it is necessary to provide a switch between the power supply output and the load to prevent the battery from keeping the load under power when the supply switch is in the off position.

You will find this circuit very useful, especially for circuits which usually operate in the untended mode. Even a near-instantaneous power interrupt will create no problems at the load, and you can always depend on having 9 V at the output.

It was previously mentioned that this circuit will protect the load from most internal power supply problems. There are a few exceptions, however. If the zener diode should open up, the full unregulated output voltage will be present across the battery terminals and at the supply output. This is the reason for including an extra zener diode (ZD_2) in the circuit. Both zeners are connected in parallel, but only the one with the lowest zener knee will actually perform the regulating function. No two zener diodes are exactly alike, and it's anybody's guess as to which one will conduct current first. In this circuit, it makes no difference. However, should one of them open up, the other one will automatically take over. This type of redundancy is not unusual in power supplies used for critical applications.

About the only thing this circuit will not protect the load from is a short circuit across the output. Assuming no extraneous pieces of metal or wire have been allowed to come in contact with the dc line, the only thing that could cause a short would be the zener diode. When zener diodes become defective, they almost always open up. On rare occasions, shorts have occurred in such components, but these incidences are so unusual that they can be disregarded altogether. Capacitors may also short out, but, again, this is quite rare. In the event of a short circuit at the output, the battery terminals would be shorted as well. This would instantly remove power from the load.

Other than the possibility of a short circuit at the output, this supply should protect all loads which require a constant 9-V operating potential. You don't have to worry about B_1 being discharged unless it is used for long periods of time with the power supply in the off position. Whenever the power supply operates, the battery will begin to charge.

One note: It may be difficult to locate a rechargeable battery with an output of exactly 9 V dc. While they are made, the type which is most available outputs an 8.4 V dc potential. In most instances, this is completely adequate to power 9-V dc circuits. However, you should change the zener diode to avoid an overcharge even by this slight amount. An RCA SK3136 or SK3749 might be better suited for rechargeable batteries with outputs of about 8.5 V.

Build the power supply circuit as you would any other. The only modification you will have to make will involve attaching a battery connector to the power supply output terminals. The battery can then be clipped in place and removed when it becomes necessary to replace it. In this type of service, a rechargeable battery should give you years of operation. This assumes that the electronic power supply will be used to provide operating current to the load during all normal operations and that the battery will be used only when a power supply failure occurs.

Incidentally, you can use this circuit as a battery charger, but never connect a standard 9-V battery to the output. Only batteries of the rechargeable type can be used, and breaking this rule could result in a fire hazard. Also, any power supply can be fitted with a backup battery to guard against supply failure. This can be done by attaching the component in an outboard fashion to the power supply output terminals.

POWER FAILURE MONITOR

In certain electronic applications, circuits are left on for long periods of time and must remain active continuously in order to accomplish their purpose. Should a power supply failure occur, these circuits may provide erroneous outputs or interrupt a timing cycle. Often, power failures are the result of temporary malfunctions and may last for only a few seconds. For example, if an ac-derived power supply is used, an overload at the power station may temporarily interrupt service, causing the electronic circuit to shut down for a short time. If the circuit is an electronic clock or other such timer, its entire purpose of operation may have been fouled without anyone ever knowing it.

Many critical electronic applications use power failure alarms which provide an indication to the technician or operator that power has been interrupted at some time before the last check was made. Such alarms are ideal in situations where circuits must be operated overnight with no attendant present. If the power failure alarm has been activated during the night, it will make the failure known the following morning when the circuit is checked.

Figure 6-56 shows a simple circuit which provides a visual indication of momentary interruptions of a power source. The circuit uses a silicon-controlled rectifier to conduct current through a small panel lamp in order to indicate a momentary failure.

The push-button switch (S_1) is a spring-loaded momentary type (normally off) which is depressed in order to turn the SCR on. This will clamp the voltage across the lamp to the forward drop of the SCR. In this circuit, the value is about 1 V and is not enough to light the lamp. In other words, the SCR is on during the normal functioning of this device, but the lamp is off. When there is a momentary power interruption which causes the 9-V supply to be turned off, the SCR also turns off and remains off. However, when line power is resumed, current must flow through the lamp because the SCR is nonconducting and forms a high resistance. This indicates that the power has been interrupted and the circuit may be reset again by momentarily depressing S_1.

The 1000-Ω resistor (R_2) clamps the gate of the sensitive SCR and prevents spurious signals from firing it. The only way to extinguish the lamp once a power failure has occurred is to close S_1 again. This causes the SCR to conduct and removes most of the power from the lamp.

All the components used to build this circuit are quite small. I used a 3-in. square section of perf board as the mounting platform. This circuit was to be mounted inside the cabinet of my ac-derived

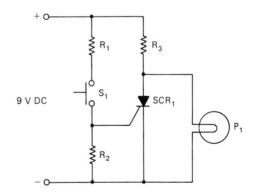

P$_1$: #47 PANEL LAMP

SCR$_1$: 276–1067 RADIO SHACK

R$_1$: 10 kΩ, $\frac{1}{2}$ W CARBON

R$_2$: 1000, $\frac{1}{2}$ W CARBON

FIGURE 6-56 Power failure monitor.   R$_3$: 33 Ω, 5 W

9-V power supply. Make certain you do not reverse the polarity of Q_1, or the lamp will light continuously.

When the circuit board is complete, connect it directly to the 9-V output of the power supply. I drilled a small hole in the top of my power supply cabinet and fitted it with a socket for the No. 47 lamp. Small lengths of insulated hookup wiring were used to connect the lamp to the SCR. Another hole was drilled to mount the reset switch, which is also connected to the circuit board with insulated hookup wire.

To test the circuit, activate the power supply. The lamp should immediately glow. If not, you either have reversed the SCR or have a defective lamp or a broken wiring connection. If the lamp does glow when the supply is activated, depress S_1. The lamp should go out. If it doesn't, examine the connections made in the gate circuit and between R_1 and the 9-V line. If the lamp goes out when S_1 is depressed, then your circuit is probably functioning as it was designed to do. The final test is made by disconnecting the power supply from the 115-V line. When you do this, nothing should happen until you reconnect power. At this time, the lamp should glow. Depressing S_1 will reset the circuit, and it will constantly monitor the 9-V output. Remember, this power supply monitor is connected in parallel with the circuit the supply drives. There will be a constant current drain from the power supply by this monitor owing to the fact that the SCR remains on until a failure causes it to stop conducting. For this reason, the monitor may not be appropriate for some battery-powered operations.

FROM 9-V BATTERY TO 6-V BATTERY

The 9-V transistor radio battery is very compact and useful as a storage device, and while the current it is capable of delivering is a bit limited, it has probably been used to power more solid-state circuits than any other type. I normally keep a sizable supply of them around my workbench in order to test and operate many of my solid-state circuits. While 9-V batteries are common, those which deliver 6 V and offer compact size are not. You generally won't find anything but a 6-V lantern battery at your local hobby store. Lantern batteries deliver high amounts of current, but this is due to their physical size, which can be detrimental in some situations.

The circuit shown in Fig. 6-57 will convert any 9-V battery into one which produces a stable 6-V output. Current drain is limited to about 50 mA, but this is all that is needed for many small projects. This is a zener diode regulator which uses a series resistor to drop

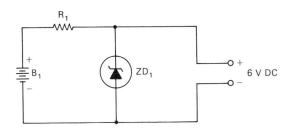

B$_1$: 9 V
R$_1$: 120 Ω, $\frac{1}{2}$ W CARBON
ZD$_1$: 6-V, $\frac{1}{2}$-W, ZENER DIODE

FIGURE 6-57 Nine-volt to 6-V conversion circuit.

the 9-V value to a nominal 6 V. The circuit is completely noncritical as long as you connect the zener as shown in the schematic drawing.

Of course, the small size of the 9-V battery is completely negated when it's necessary to wire a lot of additional circuitry to its output terminals. I overcame this problem by installing the zener regulator directly to the snap-on terminal. This is shown in Fig. 6-58. Most of these terminals consist of a piece of dielectric, through which the two connectors are inserted. The back of the terminal is usually covered with a piece of molded plastic material. All you do is snip away the plastic, taking care not to cut the terminal leads in two. When the plastic is removed, you have access to the back of the two connectors.

Clip the resistor leads as short as possible and make a solder connection to the back of the positive terminal. This is done after clipping away the positive lead (red). Prepare the zener diode in the same manner, but do not clip away the black lead from the negative connector. Solder the cathode of the zener to the remaining resistor

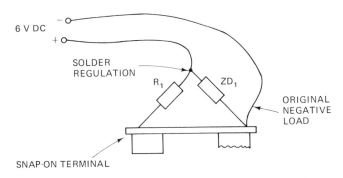

FIGURE 6-58 Wiring of battery clip for conversion circuit.

terminal. The anode is connected directly to the negative terminal clip. Now, using the severed positive lead, make a solder joint at the junction of R_1 and ZD_1. You can wrap this added circuit with a few short lengths of electrical tape to insulate the component leads.

To test the circuit, connect a dc voltmeter to the two output leads and clip the connector to any 9-V battery. The voltmeter should read a nominal 6 V dc. From now on, whenever you need a 6-V low-current supply, all that is necessary is to snap on the modified connector, and your 6 V is immediately available. When you want to revert to standard 9-V operation, use an unmodified battery connector.

Always remember to remove the 6-V connector when not in use. There will be a constant drain on the battery by this regulator circuit. This will discharge the battery after a few days. This same circuit can be modified by using a lower-value zener and a resistor with a slightly higher ohmic value. You should be able to obtain outputs of 5, 4, or even 3 V dc. Remember, however, that as you decrease the output voltage, the current drain on the battery will increase.

HIGH-VOLTAGE POWER SUPPLY

While the mass use of solid-state devices in nearly every area of the electronics industry has brought about a decrease in the use of high- and medium-voltage power supplies, there are still times when a high dc potential is needed. This is especially true in high-powered amplifiers at RF frequencies. Most often, vacuum tubes are necessary to produce high output power. Such tubes usually operate from a dc plate power supply with a potential output of 1500 V or more. This is not to say that it's not possible to produce relatively high output power using appropriate RF transistors. Indeed, several commercial amplifiers and transmitters used for radio-frequency work are 100% solid state. Solid-state amplifiers generally operate at collector potentials of no more than 100 V dc. However, the vacuum tube amplifier is the rule rather than the exception for most applications where power output exceeds 1000 W.

The basic power supply circuit shown in Fig. 6-59 is built from readily available components and will safely output up to about 4250 V dc. The filter capacitors have a combined voltage rating of 4500 V dc, so this leaves a 250-V safety margin.

This is a voltage doubler circuit whose output will be 2.8 times the transformer secondary rms. If the secondary is rated at 1000 V ac, the maximum supply output will be about 2800 V under light loading. As heavier amounts of current are drawn, the output voltage will drop to approximately 2500 V dc. Using the components specified, you will want to keep the transformer secondary rms to a

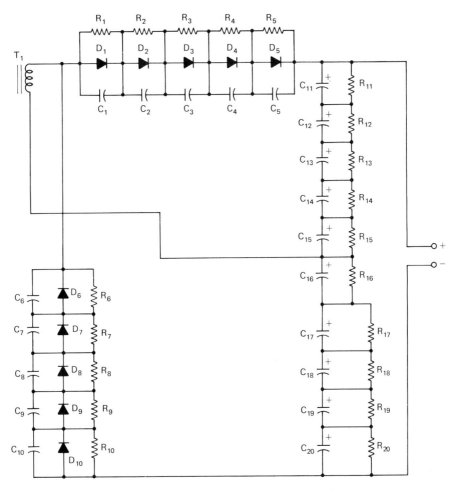

FIGURE 6-59 High-voltage power supply circuit.

value of 1500 V or less. Of course, you could input low voltage values as well. A transformer with a 6-V secondary will produce an output of about 15 V dc, but far simpler circuits can be designed for low-voltage applications. The added expense incurred in building this type of supply is justified only when you desire dc output of 2000 V or more.

The supply looks quite complex, especially when compared to a basic voltage doubler circuit which would typically use only two rectifiers, two filter capacitors, and two bleeder resistors. Electronically, this supply is just like the basic circuit. The additional components are used to keep cost to a minimum. Each of the rectifier strings is made up of five series-connected diodes. Each is rated at 1000 PRV at 1 A. In the series circuit, however, their combined rating is 5000

PRV at 1 A. You can probably purchase five of these diodes for less than 50 cents each, making the total cost of this circuit about $5 (for diodes alone). Two single-unit diodes or diode packages rated at 5000 PRV might cost $25 or more apiece.

As discussed in an earlier chapter, diodes combined in series require protective circuitry to match their internal resistance and avoid burnout due to voltage spikes. The protective circuitry for each of the two diode strings consists of parallel resistors and capacitors. While this makes the circuit more complex, these extra components are quite indispensable.

Since a full-wave voltage doubler circuit is really two half-wave rectifier circuits combined in series aiding, two separate filter capacitors are needed. High-voltage capacitors will be needed for this project, each rated at over 2000 V dc. Additionally, each capacitor should be rated to provide at least 20 μF. While oil-filled capacitors with these ratings are available, they are quite expensive and could cost more than $100 each. To avoid this expense and the problem of locating such specialized components, common electrolytic capacitors have been used in series in a similar manner as the diode strings.

Each capacitor is rated to a working voltage of 450 V dc and should possess individual capacitance ratings of at least 200 μF. Each capacitor string (C_{11}-C_{15} and C_{16}-C_{20}) is made up of five of these components in series. Series connections of capacitors bring about an increase in working voltage and a decrease in capacitance. Each string has a voltage rating of 5 times the working voltage of any one. This yields a string rated at 2250 V dc. The string capacitance value is equal to the value of one component divided by 5, or 40 μF. Each string is combined in series with the other, so the total working voltage of the 10 capacitors is 4500 V dc at a capacitance value of 20 μF. This should provide good dynamic regulation.

No transformer value is given in the schematic diagram, as this rectifier and filter circuit may be used with any type with an rms secondary value of 1500 V ac or less. The amount of output power you are able to obtain from this supply will depend on the current capability of the transformer used but is limited to a current output of approximately 800 mA owing to the 1-A rating of the silicon diode strings. Assuming a dc output of 4000 V, this configuration will yield an effective power output of 3200 W (4000 $\times$ .800). Of course, if you need higher power, you could replace D_1-D_{10} with 2-A units for an output of approximately 6500 W owing to the greater current drain which can be safely allowed. From a hobbyist-experimenter point of view, these vast amounts of power are almost never necessary. Such power supplies are often used to provide dc plate potential for amateur radio and commercial RF power amplifiers. Amateurs are limited to a maximum input power of 1000 W. At 4000

V, this would be a current drain from the supply of approximately 250 mA. Remember, this is a voltage doubler supply, so the actual current drawn from the transformer is equal to slightly more than twice that of the current drain at the dc output.

Looking again at the schematic, you will note resistors connected in parallel with each filter capacitor. These must be included in the circuit for safety and operational reasons. First, each resistor discharges the capacitor to which it is connected when the amplifier is switched off. In this mode of operation, R_{11}-R_{20} act as a string of bleeder resistors. If these were omitted from the circuit, the full dc output potential would still be present at the terminals long after the power supply was turned off. Throughout the history of electronics, many persons have been seriously injured or killed by high-voltage power supplies that were turnd off and completely disconnected from primary power.

During the operation of the power supply, these same resistors serve much the same purpose as R_1-R_{10}. They minimize internal resistance differences within the filter capacitors, making certain that each drops an equal share of the total output voltage. Without these matching resistors, one capacitor might drop 1000 V, while the others would each drop 300 V or so. The 1000-V drop across a single capacitor is more than double its maximum working voltage. By omitting R_{11}-R_{20}, you are asking for trouble, both from an operational and, more importantly, a safety standpoint.

Also from a safety standpoint, construction is quite critical. Looking at electronic operation alone, the circuit will probably work regardless of how you slap it together. But you must remember that a high-voltage dc power supply is a lethal device, once which doesn't produce mild shocks. Rather, when you come in contact with 3000 or 4000 V, you are quite lucky to be alive after the experience. Because of the safety factor, this project is recommended only to persons who have had a fair amount of building experience and realize the mortal danger of human contact with such potentials.

Begin construction by installing the rectifier circuit on a 6-in. square section of perforated circuit board. Figure 6-60 shows a suggested component layout. Don't try to squeeze the circuit into a much smaller package. Most dc power supplies of this type will require a rather large power transformer, and the capacitor bank may take up even more space, so there is really very little to be gained by shrinking the size of the rectifier strings. Then, too, it may be necessary to replace a rectifier now and then, so the increased size of this circuit board and component layout will better facilitate this operation. Each rectifier is mounted to the board by inserting the leads through appropriate perforations. The protection circuit consisting of a $\frac{1}{2}$-W resistor and a disk-ceramic capacitor is installed on

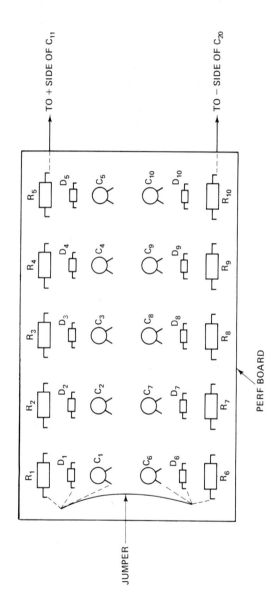

FIGURE 6-60 Component layout for rectifier board.

either side of the mounted diode. This process is repeated for all 10 rectifiers. When all components have been mounted, twist the leads together and solder. Each solder connection will actually consist of six separate leads, as the resistor, capacitor, and diode combinations are joined together. As you can see from the schematic, this will yield contact points for the power transformer and the capacitor string.

This circuit board may now be set aside temporarily. The next portion of construction involves mounting the filter capacitors and matching-bleeder resistors. This is going to take a bit of mechanical know-how, but there are several ways proper mounting can be accomplished. You must always remember that each filter capacitor is insulated to slightly over its working voltage rating. Since each capacitor is rated at 450 working volts, this means the potential between the positive terminal and the negative one must not be higher than this value *and* this potential must be maintained to within specified limits between the positive contact and circuit ground. If you look at the schematic, the following discussion will be a bit clearer.

Only one capacitor in the 10-component string has its negative terminal connected to circuit ground (the negative dc output). C_{11} (at the top of the string) has the full dc output potential at its positive terminal. It drops a maximum of 450 V of this total potential, while C_{12} takes the next 450 V (or one-tenth of the total output potential), and so on, to the bottom of the string. C_{20} has its negative contact at power supply ground potential, but its positive terminal is at a potential of one-tenth of the total output (450 V dc maximum). If you place a dc voltmeter across each capacitor, you will obtain a reading of one-tenth of the total output voltage.

So far this discussion has involved common power supply theory. However, let's move further into this circuit. A voltmeter placed at the positive and negative output terminals will read the full dc output potential. The positive terminal is connected directly to the top of C_{11}, while the negative terminal is connected directly to the bottom of C_{20}. This means that between the top of C_{11} and the power supply ground, the full power supply potential exists. C_{11} is only dropping a maximum of 450 V, *but* if its metal case is grounded (to the chassis or negative output lead), 10 times this voltage will exist within this same component. Therefore, every capacitor in the string must have its metal body (which is usually its negative electrode contact) insulated from the power supply chassis ground and from the metal bodies of all other capacitors. Some electrolytic capacitors are equipped with a thin vinyl cover to act as an insulator. The insulation rating here is still not much higher than the working voltage rating. You can't depend on insulation rated to withstand 500 V dc or so to withstand 3000 V or more. Make absolutely certain

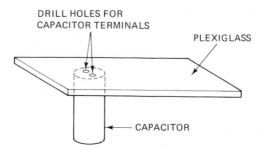

FIGURE 6-61 Electrolytic capacitor layout.

that none of the capacitor bodies (insulated or otherwise) are allowed to come in contact with each other or with the power supply ground. The only exception here would be C_{20}, the negative terminal of which serves as the supply ground.

Electrolytic capacitors of the type used in this circuit are far too large to be mounted on perf board. In my circuit, I used a 1.5-ft length of $\frac{1}{4}$-in. plexiglass about 5 in. wide for mounting purposes. My capacitors contained screw-in top-mounted terminals, so the plexiglass strip was drilled to accept the terminal bolts. Each capacitor was suspended from the plexiglass, keeping all components out of contact of the chassis and each other. A pictorial representation of this is shown in Fig. 6-61. If you use capacitors with standard axial-mounted leads, the arrangement shown in Fig. 6-62 may be more appropriate. Epoxy cement is used to bond each component to the plexiglass sheeting. The resistors are then connected to the capacitor terminals. Try to suspend the carbon bodies away from the plexiglass, as bleeder resistors can heat up and possibly melt the material.

You may now begin to combine the two major portions of the circuit. It will first be necessary to install the power transformer in

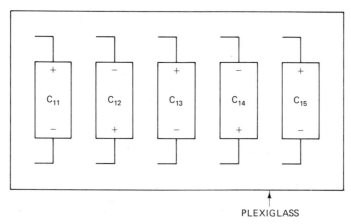

FIGURE 6-62 Capacitor layout using components with axial leads.

an appropriate enclosure and wire the primary circuit. Once this has been done, mount the rectifier circuit board in close proximity with the transformer secondary leads. Ceramic insulating posts are used to suspend the circuit board from the metal chassis. Before making any connections at this point, install the capacitor bank within the chassis as well. The plexiglass is a good insulator, but make certain you use mounting techniques which keep all capacitors away from the metal chassis and cover. Figure 6-63 shows how I arranged my supply.

Connect one lead of the power transformer secondary to the junction of D_1 and D_6. The other power supply lead connects to the center of the capacitor bank. Now, using insulated hookup wire, make a short connection between the output of D_5 and the positive terminal of C_{11}. Another piece of hookup wire is used to connect the bottom of D_{10} to the bottom of C_{20}. Your supply chassis should be fitted with a high-voltage output connector. Two more lengths of hookup wire access the top of C_{11} and the bottom of C_{20}.

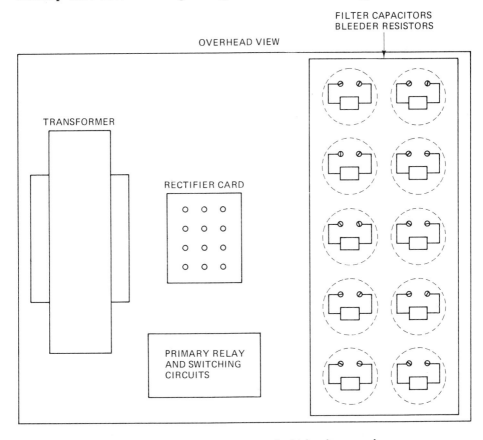

FIGURE 6-63 Component arrangement for high-voltage supply.

Your circuit is now complete, but go over everything one more time, making sure all hookup wiring leads are correct and are not touching the chassis, enclosure wall, or other components. If all seems to be in order, connect the probes of an appropriate voltmeter to the dc output terminals and activate the power switch. Your voltage reading should be equal to about 2.8 times the rms secondary value.

This is a fairly complex project, and, again, it is not intended for beginners to electronic project building. The supply does go together rather nicely, because most of the components are relatively large, and only a small amount of miniaturized wiring is involved. Safety has been stressed throughout the discussion of this project, but a little more needs to be said. If your power supply does not work the first time, then it will be necessary to go back into the circuit in order to find the problem. Be extremely wary here. A defective power supply can be especially dangerous, because a wiring error can sometimes negate the safety features which have been built in. When you go into the circuit again, make sure the ac power cord has been removed from the wall outlet and assume that the filter capacitors are charged to their maximum potential. Carefully make a voltage check at each capacitor, and use a screwdriver with an insulated handle to short out each one. This will ensure that no stored energy remains within these components.

Be wary also when taking voltage readings. Many inexpensive voltmeters may contain high-voltage scales, but sometimes the probes are not insulated to withstand these potentials. I don't like touching any wire, even when adequately insulated, which is a potential high-voltage contact. The best thing to do is fix the probes to the output terminals in such a manner that you don't have to hold them in place. You may then activate the power supply and note the reading on the meter from a short distance away.

My power supply was designed to provide plate potential to a linear amplifier used in my amateur radio endeavors. The transformer used contained a 1000-V secondary, bringing about a dc output of just under 2800 V. The total effective capacitance is 20 μF, and this provides good dynamic regulation, even for rather critical high-voltage applications. For similar types of work, I think you will find this supply to be more than adequate.

REGULATED TRI-VOLTAGE POWER SUPPLY

In today's electronics market, one can often find a reasonably good buy on dc power supplies. Most of these are basic circuits which do not contain any form of electronic regulation. As such, they may not be able to properly operate some solid-state circuits. These power supplies usually contain only a power transformer, a rectifier, and a filter capacitor or choke filter. The stated output of these supplies will vary depending on the amount of current which is drawn. Most solid-state circuits which are to be driven by a power supply require better voltage stability than these inexpensive units are capable of delivering.

For a few extra dollars, you can add a circuit to these power supplies which will stabilize the voltage to within respectable limits. This allows for a far more versatile application. The circuit shown in Fig. 6-64 is a basic zener diode regulator which has incorporated a three-position rotary switch to allow for three different output voltages. The values of the zener diodes are not specified in the schematic drawing, because many different combinations are possible and the builder will choose those which will produce output voltages that conform to individual needs. Using $\frac{1}{2}$-W zeners and a 5-W adjustable resistor, the supply should be capable of safely delivering about 250 mA of current to the load. The rotary switch should contain contacts which are rated to withstand a current of at least 500 mA in order to provide an adequate safety margin.

In my circuit, I used an adjustable wire-wound resistor for R_1. This was an Allied Electronics No. 880-1050. It sells for about $1.50. Alternately, you could use a rheostat in order to make adjustments a little easier. The Allied Electronics 875-4010 can serve as a direct replacement. Actually, once the resistor is initially set, it may not be necessary to make further adjustments as long as the zener diode voltages are not widely diversified.

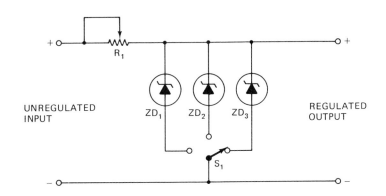

R₁ : 0.50 Ω, 12 W ADJUSTABLE

S₁ : 3-POSITION ROTARY SWITCH

ZD₁-ZD₃ : SEE TEXT

FIGURE 6-64 Trivoltage regulator circuit.

This circuit is designed to be incorporated in an existing power supply chassis, and it is not necessary to use a separate piece of perf board as the mounting platform. The rotary switch is installed through the front panel of the power supply, and the zeners are connected across the contacts and directly to the positive dc voltage output line or terminal of the power supply. The movable switch contact is connected to the dc ground of the original power supply. The zeners are not in the circuit until the switch is engaged. This grounds out the base of a single diode, the circuit is completed, and a regulated output is obtained. In some instances, it may be necessary to tie the positive leads of the zener diodes together and connect them to the positive output of the power supply with a short length of insulated hookup wire. Make certain the diodes are installed as shown. If you should reverse any of them, that particular circuit leg will not operate.

To test the circuit, connect a dc voltmeter across the output terminals. Set R_1 to the midrange position (about 25 Ω) and activate the supply. Let's assume that S_1 is connected to a zener diode rated at 9 V. Your power supply output should read 9 V. If the value is higher than this, increase the resistance of R_1. You should see the meter suddenly drop to the 9-V value. Now advance the rotary switch to the next zener diode. Chances are you will not have to adjust R_1 further. In every case, the output voltage from the unregulated power supply should be about 3 V higher than the desired regulated output. Most unregulated 12-V supplies really output nearly 18 V, so you may have the capability of choosing a regulated output of as high as 15 V dc. I used 1-W zener diodes with this supply, although $\frac{1}{2}$-W units should also do the job. If the unregulated output voltage is far higher than the desired regulated output, it may be necessary to replace R_1 with a 100-Ω unit. This will limit the amount of output current which can be drawn to about 100 mA.

This circuit may also be used as an outboard device by installing it in a separate metal enclosure using basically the same mounting techniques. It is so small, however, that even the smaller power supply chassis will usually offer more than enough room to accommodate it.

Warning: When switching between zener diodes, make certain the electronic load is completely disconnected from this supply. During the switching procedure, the full unregulated output can be present at the regulated output terminals. This circuit was specifically designed for operation with an unregulated 12-V supply whose output was over 17.5 V. Other supplies with higher output voltages may require a different series resistor and probably one with a 20-W power rating. Using this circuit with my 12-V supply, I have been able to obtain regulated outputs of 15, 12, and 9 V dc using three zener diodes rated at these same values, respectively.

ANOTHER TRI-VOLTAGE ZENER DIODE SUPPLY

The preceding project involved a zener diode regulator circuit which would output three different dc potentials. This was accomplished using zeners, each of which was rated at a different value. A similar circuit is shown in Fig. 6-65. This is also a tri-voltage supply, but it uses three identical zener diodes in a switched series circuit. When I designed this supply, I needed a low-current power source which would deliver an output of up to 9 V dc. All I had on hand were three zener diodes, all of which were rated at 3 V dc. I needed a supply which would deliver a 6-V dc output at about 50 to 60 mA. This was quite possible with the components I had on hand, since zener diodes may be wired in series to bring about a different zener knee or regulating value. A single 3-V zener diode will conduct current at a fraction over the 3-V value. Two such units in series will add values and conduct at 6 V. All three zener diodes in series will be the equivalent of one 9-V zener ($3 \times 3 = 9$).

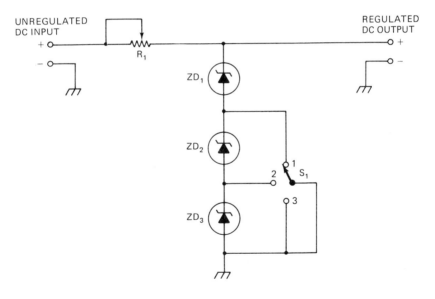

S$_1$: 3-POSITION ROTARY SWITCH

R$_1$: 0–200-Ω, 2-W POTENTIOMETER

ZD$_1$-ZD$_3$: 3-W, 1-W ZENER DIODE (RCA   SK3838/5065A)

FIGURE 6-65 Trivoltage regulator circuit using series-connected zener diodes.

Since a three-position rotary switch was already on hand, I decided to build a variable output supply, one which would deliver a regulated 3-, 6-, or 9-V dc output. The circuit shown switches zener diodes as did the previous supply. However, the difference lies in the fact that these components are not always switched in and out of the circuit but in and out of the series string. Looking at the schematic drawing, when S_1 is in the No.3 position, all three diodes are in the circuit, and the output is 9 V dc. When S_1 is rotated to the No. 2 position, ZD_3 is shorted out, leaving only ZD_1 and ZD_2 in the circuit. This provides a 6-V output. Finally, in the No. 1 position, ZD_2 and ZD_3 are shorted out, leaving a single diode in the circuit for a 3-V dc output.

The series resistor was a 2-W unit I had on hand. If you draw only small amounts of current, a $\frac{1}{2}$- or 1-W unit may suffice. It will probably not be necessary to make adjustments to this component when switching between 9 and 6 V dc. However, you will have to increase the resistance for a 3-V output to prevent the zener from drawing excessive amounts of current. If the resistance is too low, more current must be conducted by the zener diode string in order to effect the appropriate voltage drop. All three regulated outputs may be obtained with a minimum dc input (unregulated) of 12 V.

This circuit may be built on perf board and installed in an existing unregulated power supply. Alternately, the perf board may be mounted in a separate aluminum enclosure to be used as an outboard device for many different types of power supplies. Construction is quite simple in that only the zener diodes are mounted to the board. The variable resistor and S_1 will be mounted through the wall of the enclosure, using hookup wire to make the appropriate connection to the diodes.

Checkout is handled in the same manner as with the previous project. Start with S_1 in the No. 3 position and connect a dc voltmeter to the output terminals. With an input voltage of at least 12 V dc, activate the circuit and note the reading on the voltmeter. Adjust R_1, if necessary, to obtain the correct dc output. This involves backing off on the resistance just to the point where the 9-V value is obtained. Then connect the output of the supply to the load and adjust again. A 9-V output obtained under no-load conditions may not hold up when current is being drawn, so all adjustments should be made with the load connected. Repeat this process for the 6- and 3-V positions and mark the correct setting of R_1 on the panel through which this component is mounted. In actual operation, you will automatically rotate R_1 to the correct position for the output desired. It will also be necessary to adjust and mark S_1 in the same manner.

While this was originally designed as a low-current supply, much higher amounts of power may be drawn from this circuit by replacing R_1 with a 12-W 0-100-Ω rheostat. Your unregulated dc power supply must be able to output at least 30% more than the current drawn from the regulated circuit.

HALF-WAVE VOLTAGE TRIPLER

Half-wave voltage multiplier circuits are not recommended for connection directly to the ac line due to the electrical shock hazard. However, they may be safely used with power transformers and will allow unused transformer windings to supply operating current at much higher voltages than their ac rms. Figure 6-66 shows a voltage tripler circuit which is composed of three half-wave power supplies connected in series. I used this circuit at the output of a 6.3-V transformer winding to deliver 25 V dc to a surplus relay. The power transformer was pulled from an old television receiver, and the windings were used for other purposes within the device I was building. This was an amateur radio transmitter, and the antenna changeover relay required approximately 25 V at a moderate current. The 6.3-V secondary winding of the power transformer was rated at 3 A and had more than enough power capability to drive the relay. The only problem was the voltage. A voltage tripler circuit provides a peak dc output of more than 3 times the rms secondary value. In practice, the multiplication factor is more like 4.2 times rms, but under load this

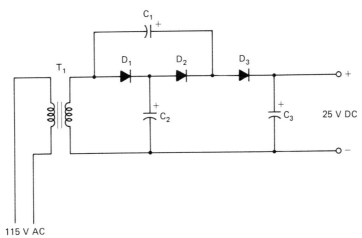

C_1-C_2-C_3: 500 μF, 50 V DC
D_1-D_2-D_3: 100 PIV, 1 A SILICON
T_1: 115 V PRIMARY, 6.3 V SECONDARY (500 MA)

FIGURE 6-66   Half-wave voltage tripler circuit.

value will drop a bit. I was able to throw the circuit together from components I had in my junk box.

A 6-in. square section of perf board was used to mount all components. I had plenty of space, so I was not terribly concerned about physical size, although this circuit could be substantially reduced by mounting the components closer together and using a smaller section of perf board. Wiring is not critical, but you must be sure to get the polarities of the diodes and electrolytic capacitors right.

A half-wave voltage doubler connects one side of the transformer winding directly to the load. Two of the filter capacitors are also connected to this point. If the ground side of the circuit is to be the chassis (as in my case), installation is simplified. I simply grounded one lead from the 6.3-V winding to the chassis and connected the other lead to the D_1 input. The output at D_3 was connected to the positive relay terminal. The other terminal was grounded (along with the negative leads of C_2 and C_3) to the chassis. Under no-load conditions, the dc output was nearly 27 V, but with the relay connected and engaged, the value dropped a few volts. While my home-brew transmitter is not used very much these days, whenever it is put on the air, the relay circuit is still fully operational.

You can use this same circuit with a 5-V winding to obtain an output of about 20 V peak. Some transformers have center-tapped 5-V windings, so by using the center tap in one lead to drive the voltage tripler, you can obtain an output of about 10 V. You can also use this circuit with a 12-V winding, but it would be a good idea to replace C_3 with a capacitor rated at 100 V dc. The output from a 12-V winding would be slightly in excess of the 50-V maximum rating.

This voltage tripler circuit actually increases the rms voltage by over 4 times, so you must remember that you can draw only one-fourth of the current that this winding is rated to deliver. The schematic specifies a 500-mA secondary winding, which should allow you to safely draw up to 125 mA. Higher amounts of current may be drawn by using a more powerful transformer, but the diodes will not withstand more than about 800 mA.

Index

Scrambler project, 108-9
Screwdrivers, 36, 38
Self-driven strength meter project, 115-19
Semiconductor junctions, 1-13
    current flow in *N*-type material, 5-6
    current flow in *P*-type material, 6-7
    N-type germanium, 2-3
    PN junctions, 7-13
    P-type germanium, 3-5
Semiconductors, defined, 1
Series diode protection circuit project, 83
Series rectifier configurations, 22-25
Signal diodes, 13
    electrical characteristics of, 14
    schematic diagram for, 15
    thermal damage, 29
Silicon, 1
Silicon-controlled rectifiers, 14, 23, 66-72
    examples of, 67
    lighting sensor project, 105-7
    light-triggered switch project, 102-5
    uses of, 70-72
    voltage-current characteristics of, 68-70
6-V batteries, conversion of 9-V batteries to, 154-56
Solder, 31-32
Soldering station, 28-29
Soldering technique, 28-32
Solid-state diode projects (*See* Projects)
Strobeflash slave adapter project, 93-95
Switch projects:
    crystal, 98-100
    light-triggered SCR, 102-5
    two-position illumination, 79-81
    two-state light switch-dimmer, 81-82
    voice-activated, 100-102

T

Test instruments, 36-38
Thermal damage, 29
Thermal protection, 29-30, 32-33
Thyristors, 66-73
    defined, 66

Thyristors (*cont.*)
    diacs, 73
    silicon-controlled rectifiers (*See* Silicon-controlled rectifiers)
    triacs (*See* Triacs)
Tools, 36, 38-39
Transformerless power supply project, 146-48
Triacs:
    construction project, 91-93
    defined, 72-73
    voice-actuated switch project, 100-102
Trivalent impurities, 2, 3, 4, 7
Tri-voltage (regulated) power supply projects, 164-69
Tuning diodes, 16-17
Two-position illumination switch project, 79-81
Two-state light switch-dimmer project, 81-82

V

Varactor diodes, 16-18
Voice-actuated switch project, 100-102
Voltage doubler:
    add-on circuit project, 43-46
    full-wave, 61
    half-wave, 60-61
Voltage indicator (LED) project, 128-31
Voltage meter (line) project, 126-28
Voltage multipliers, 59-65
    doubler (*See* Voltage doubler)
    quadrupler, 64-65
    tripler (*See* Voltage tripler)
Voltage supplies, combinational, 56-59
Voltage tripler, 62-64
    half-wave project, 169-70
Voltmeter projects:
    ac-dc, 125-26
    dummy antenna RF, 121-23
VU meter (LED) project, 137, 138

W

Work area, 41
Workbench, 36
Work habits, 39-41

Z

Zener diodes, 13
  electrical characteristics, 15
  knee test circuit project, 109-11

Zener diodes (*cont.*)
  overvoltage protection projects,
   89-91
  schematic symbols for, 15